LITTLE WEKIVA
MEMORIES

LITTLE WEKIVA
MEMORIES

Kayaking & other adventures

NICHOLE DELAFIELD-BROMME
LEIF BROMME

Little Wekiva Memories
By Nichole Delafield-Bromme and Leif Bromme
Artwork by Nichole Delafield Bromme and Leif Bromme
Book Design by James Monroe Design LLC.
All photographs are from the authors' collections unless otherwise noted.
This book is typeset using the fonts: Adobe Garamond and Florida
(originally designed by Hans Möhring in 1931).

Hastings House Publishers/Newhouse Creative Group
Orlando, Florida
HastingsHousePublishers.com
©2025, Nichole Delafield Bromme and Leif Bromme

Names: Delafield-Bromme, Nichole | Bromme, Leif | Monroe, James, Book Designer
Title: Little Wekiva Memories / by Nichole Delafield-Bromme and Leif Bromme
Description: Orlando, FL | Hastings House, 2025. | Series: Kayaking Adventures | Summary: Explore
    Florida's Little Wekiva through photos, art, and the authors' kayak adventures.
Identifiers: ISBN 979-8-9936590-0-8 (paperback)
    978-1-945493-80-5 (Ultra Color Paperback)
    978-1-945493-82-9 (Hardcover)
Subjects: LCSH: Little Wekiva. | Florida. | Kayaking. | Travel. | Outdoors. |
Classification: LCC GV191.2.D45 Lit 2025 (print)

All rights reserved. No part of this publication may be reproduced, stored or transmitted in any form or by any means, electronic, mechanical, photocopying, recording, scanning, or otherwise without written permission from the publisher. It is illegal to copy this book, post it to a website, or distribute it by any other means without permission.

To Sue Tyndall, our dear friend, who helped us discover
the beauty and mystery of Florida.

CONTENTS

Introduction | 1

Springs: Basic Highlights Defined by Leif 2

Our Story: Getting to Know Florida—Nichole 5

Adventures On The Little Wekiva River: Discovering The Springs,
Sanlando, Palm, Starbuck, Ginger Ale, and Pegasus—Leif 33

    Introduction 33

    Sanlando Springs 34

    Palm Springs 46

    Starbuck Spring 59

    Ginger Ale Springs 64

    Pegasus Spring 70

LIFE ALONG THE LITTLE WEKIVA: Leif and I join countless others who have found the Little Wekiva River and its tributaries to be beautifully mysterious—Nichole.. 81

    Robin Sheldon. 82

    Don and Virginia Barker. 98

    Sandra Smith Regal. 104

    Mayanne Downs. 108

    John Rountree. 116

    Ron and Lisa Huston 120

    Billy Ridgeback Bodie. 129

    Parker Wilson 135

Acknowledgments | 154

Notes | 156

Bibliography | 159

v

INTRODUCTION

Life is an adventure! With any good adventure, there are surprises along the way that make the journey sweeter. Exploring the five springs flowing into the Little Wekiva River, over a one-mile stretch in Longwood, Florida, has been a journey full of surprises for Nichole and her son, Leif. Moving to Florida was an adventure for the entire Bromme family. Acclimating to what felt like a strange new land was unnerving at times, especially for Nichole. Plant life took on different shapes, black bears roamed freely, and alligators lurked in murky waters. Leif, on the other hand, dove into his new surroundings with energy. He would drop to all fours with the excitement of a two-year-old, chasing after tiny frogs hopping in the grass. As Leif grew, he spent more time kayaking on the Little Wekiva River, its tributaries, and the beautiful springs that feed it. The river became his starting point for adventures with family and friends. These adventures helped their entire family grow to love the distinct beauty of Florida.

The Wekiva River Basin in Central Florida includes the Little Wekiva that meanders into the larger Wekiva River, which then flows into the St. Johns. Continuing North, the St. Johns River travels through the Ocala National Forest and on up to the city of Jacksonville, where it finally empties into the Atlantic Ocean. The forests surrounding the Wekiva River are home to black bears, panthers, coyotes, even a few monkeys. A lovely, one mile stretch of the Little Wekiva River in Seminole County is dotted with five springs: Sanlando, Palm, Ginger Ale, Pegasus, and Starbuck. Come along with Leif and Nichole as they kayak, hunt for treasure, and explore these beautiful springs. Their journey of discovery unearths mysteries of the natural world and shares unforgettable stories of people who live their lives along the banks of the Little Wekiva River.

Birds Eye view of the Little Wekiva River

Springs
Basic Highlights Defined by Leif

Springs, as our portals to the aquifer, are important environmental filters. They help to keep Florida's water systems fresh and clean. The following terms describe components of Florida springs.

Spring: "A point of focused discharge of groundwater"—Saint Johns River Management District.

Artesian Springs: Locations where water is pushed through karst due to pressure. Aquifer water is forced to the surface as rainwater replaces it underground. Elevation changes also contribute to the pressures that force groundwater to the surface.

Aquifer: A layer of water underneath Florida's limestone layer that is replenished from rainfall. These waters are the source of our springs.

Boil: A spring discharge that causes visual turbulence on the surface of the water.

Karst: The porous limestone layer underneath Florida, punctuated by pockets of water and sections of the aquifer.

Magnitude: The measure of a spring's daily water discharge. First magnitude springs produce upwards of 65 million gallons of water a day. Each magnitude thereafter produces less water, descending all the way to small 8th magnitude springs.

Pool: The basin surrounding a spring vent that collects most of the outflow. The spring run flows out from the pool. Some springs do not have pools due to the topography of their locations.

Run: The stream that connects a karst spring to another body of water, allowing spring water to enter the water system.

Saint Johns River Water Management District (SJRWMD): The state organization that manages Florida's river water, tributaries, springs, and aquifers.

Sand Boil: A spring discharge caused by water pressure pushing through a layer of sand.

Seep Springs: Locations where water "seeps" into areas of lower elevation due to the elevation difference in the water table rather than internal aquifer pressure.

Sinkholes: Dissolved areas of karst that resemble springs because the surface has collapsed into a layer of the aquifer.

Vent: A gap in the limestone layer that allows pressurized water from the aquifer to make its way to the surface.

Weir: A low dam built across a river to raise the level of water upstream or regulate its flow.

The Springs: Refers to the community developed by Earl Downs in the early 1970s.

the springs: Refers to the water flowing from the aquifers into the Little Wekiva River.

Sand Boil

Our Story
Getting to Know Florida
—Nichole

Have you ever felt that your life was a bit like a page turner, full of surprising storylines? A surprising chapter in our family's story was a move to Florida. We didn't see that plot twist coming. Everything in Florida seemed unfamiliar to us. Blinding sun. Heat that hits you like a Mack truck. Humidity that drains every ounce of energy from you. Plant and animal life that seemed threatening.

    I started each day in surroundings that felt otherworldly. A throbbing hum, this insistent clicking, greeted me when I stepped outside. Hemmed in by dense foliage, my senses were on high alert. I was conscious of creatures communicating all around me. Leif, my son, told me I was hearing a mating call sung by male Cicadas. Each species has its own distinctive song that attracts only females of its kind. The synchronized, plaintive chorus is a group effort to procreate. I felt their persistent buzz and whirl like a rattle in my brain. The noise surged to a level I could hear over the engine of my car as I drove under live oaks whose snake-like branches coiled and twisted in the shade of their small, sturdy leaves. This dark canopy battles for dominance with curtains of moss draped in the crooks of those serpentine branches. Ferns and bromeliads cling to the bark. Dark tree shadows play on the bleached asphalt, hinting at deeper color, long faded.

LITTLE WEKIVA MEMORIES

OUR STORY

In the cocoon of my car, I found a great place to reflect. There was a lot to take in. That faded pavement, the gray moss, gray-brown tree trunks, and branches tinged pink, white, and gray-green from fungal growth. Up north in Minnesota, where our family was from, and along the Eastern seaboard that we came to call home, the landscapes are a vivid, Granny Smith green. My artist eyes saw a different color palette here. Florida seemed to be painted in a wash tinted with gray tones. At times the sun shone so brightly that I felt like I was living in an overexposed photograph.

My eyes were also drawn to the skies. Florida clouds stack up like skyscrapers. Sometimes I imagine them as puffs of steam escaping from a speeding engine, or a bubble machine working on overdrive.

"Will you look at those clouds?" I exclaimed. "Aren't they unusual? Just look at those colors!"

"Mom, can you stop talking about the clouds?"

I realized my children were right, this observation of mine was becoming repetitive. Soon I was met with a silence. Catching the three of them in my rearview mirror, I saw the roll of their eyes. They would turn their faces and gaze out the window, looking away from me and the sky, refusing to engage in a cloud conversation. But soon, their eyes would drift upwards again, and they knew, as I did, that these clouds were like nothing we'd seen before. Clouds roll in from the Gulf of Mexico and blow in from the Atlantic, crashing into each other above central Florida. They pile up, overlap, explode in layers of sun-kissed white, gray, and ominous black. Dark storm clouds with sun-drenched, cotton-ball white fronts surprise you with terrific downpours. You can quickly drive in and out of these torrential showers as if you're slipping through a swinging door.

Back when my husband Jeff first got that call from the corporate recruiter, I thought we were heading to Disney World, where everything would revolve around Mickey. I realize now how misguided I was. Now I know the Magic Kingdom has been carefully cultivated and curated by a round-the-clock landscape crew who has beaten the "real Florida" into submission. The "real Florida" is a different kind of world. I found myself uncomfortably transplanted into that wild, untamed land, full of scrub brush, sand, and palms, of which there are many! Again, with help from Leif and his

ever-growing list of palm trees, I learned there are some 2,500 different species of palm trees in the world. Almost all of them can be grown in Florida. Experts say there are twelve palm trees native to Florida. We have buccaneer palms, royal palms, and bottle palms, whose trunks really do look just like wine bottles. There are thatch palms, saw palmetto, and Everglades palms that love the marshy wetlands of Southern Florida.

In addition to the endless variety of plant life in Florida, you can find every manner of creature lurking in the thick undergrowth. I wasn't prepared for all the bugs and other creepy crawlies. When you're new to Florida, natives seem to enjoy injecting a little fright into your thin Floridian skin.

"Watch out for alligators. They'll come right up in your backyard from that there crick. You'd better check under your car. Gaters'll hide there and grab your leg when you're trying to open your door."

The man who cleaned our gutters warned, "You have banana spiders all around your windows. I don't want to get near those things; they'll do a number on you. They have a nasty bite." Then there are the roaches. I can handle a lot of things, but a cockroach always gives me the heebie-jeebies. I've grabbed a broom and swept a snake out of the house, and I could be persuaded that a little mouse has a cuteness factor. But a ROACH is not welcome — ever! My first order of business after the moving van pulled away was to call the exterminator. We were soon on a first name basis. Guillermo would

repeatedly work me into his schedule. Guillermo, wherever you are now, thank you.

Often, when I walked outside, I'd smell decay. This seemed odd as all around me I saw lush, verdant plant-life. The intense rain and humidity, however, create a perfect petri dish for growing and decomposing. I was positive I could see things sprouting before my eyes. It seemed that rain induced six inches of new growth overnight. Back home, in that distant idyl, I trimmed my azaleas once after their spring bloom, yet Florida azaleas demanded four or more trimmings that first year. A few flowers survived my incessant clipping, but none of the bushes bloomed like those magnificent bursts of color from our Virginia azaleas. I became a quick study. One savage pruning after the bloom (which is tricky to discern since they bud and bloom sporadically from November to May) is all I'll allow. My heart broke after that first brutal clipping. All that remained was 24-inch stalks with barely a green leaf to be found. In a few weeks time, lush new growth filled in. I was amazed and relieved. We learned to beat back the jungle and keep the area around our house somewhat tame which gave the yard a free-spirited vibe. Along the side of our property and down by the creek, native brush and bramble rage in full force. Trees fall, branches break, plants collapse into the ground, creating thickets filled with moisture that pull this organic litter into itself, making a happy home for fungi and larvae to grow. Slugs, millipedes, beetles, spiders, and snakes hide, raccoon families forage for food and opossum slink about in the dark.

View through screen with bears

Bobcat

The occasional bobcat, panther, and alligator all call this jungle and waterway home. Bears, lots of them, make it their serious business to keep the animal trails cleared through the undergrowth. All of this kept me out of our backyard; it felt hostile.

During those early years in Florida, I stayed safely protected on our screened-in porch and gazed out at this foreign land. Looking at the dense growth lining a wide expanse of weedy grass to the creek, I was conflicted. I knew the creek was special. From afar, I'd gaze at the swiftly moving water of the Little Wekiva River running along the back edge of our property. The problem was that I was just scared of all that might be lurking in and around it. Occasionally, we would see people paddling by in a canoe or I would notice a figure bent over in the water. I could hear the old children's rhyme in my head: "One of these things is not like the other." The dancing ball would bounce from object to object. I compared myself with this figure in the water who appeared so at ease, and I would think of others I'd met who seemed so different from me. Would I ever fit in here? The dancing ball landed firmly on me when the song ended. I was different. I didn't belong. Everything felt foreign and uncomfortable.

From the distance of the house, the figure in the water appeared to be a woman —a naked woman —moving with ease back and forth in the water. "What?! She couldn't be out in that creek totally unprotected from all that lived there. Didn't she know she needed to take precautions?" Danger lurks in those waters: snakes, alligators, and who knows what else. She needed the kind of protection that only high-wading boots, long pants, hat, gloves, and a bear horn attached to her hip could give. After all, that's what I layered on the few times I'd ventured to the creek's edge. Curiosity got the better of me, so I pulled on my boots and headed for the creek. I was going to meet this unusual woman—naked or not. Embarrassment crept in as I got closer to the creek; this could be awkward. The woman was leaning over a rake, fully intent on her work. I called out a hello. Raising her head, she turned to greet me and smiled. Her weathered, brown face, body and bathing suit were all the same color! The current moved quickly, swirling around her ankles as she stood in the shallows. The water was so clear. I could see white swaths of sand alternating with deep green, velvety bands of algae waving beneath the surface. She offered a sheepish apology for being on our side of the fence. Introducing herself as Sue, she went on to explain that she was attacking the algae and other plant life growing near the bank as this helped to keep the water moccasins from making nests along the shore. She seemed so nonchalant and underdressed for breaking up water moccasin nests. Sue went on to explain that the previous owner hadn't minded her working in the water. She continued, telling me how much she loved being out there in that spring-fed stream, "Who needs therapy when you have the creek to play in."

LITTLE WEKIVA MEMORIES

View up-river near Starbuck Spring

Standing there by the water's edge, drenched in sunlight, I found it easy to talk to Sue. Watching little fish swirl in the shallows, I felt my shoulders loosen. Crawdads scooted away from Sue's rake, their little hind legs working overtime, pushing them toward new hiding places. I traced leaves as they floated by, watching them disappear around the bend in the river. Sue shared details about the spring bubbling in our neighbor's back yard and the river water that joins it. She encouraged me to take a closer look, so I sloshed my boots into the water.

Standing next to her, gazing upstream, I was captivated by a tunnel-like canopy created from a jumble of plant life. A narrow corridor of water flowed through the woods. Sunlight escaped the dense cover here and there, painting golden splotches of color on the water's surface. I could see a distinct fork in the river. Sue explained that a clear, spring-fed pool was releasing a continuous flow of water into one fork. The other fork was formed by the Little Wekiva River. The two flow as one, passing by us in varied depths depending on seasons and storms. Heavy rains will add run-off water to the river, changing the flow and shifting the balance of spring-to-river water. The clear water then turns into caramel tones. I felt like I was learning a new language—the river's language.

Gar fish

The magic all around me teased my senses. I reached down and trailed my fingers in the cool, refreshing water. Peering into the water, I noticed channels carved deep in the sand where fish played. Tiny minnows darted about. I caught myself smiling. Then a huge fish, long and narrow, with a pointed snout raced by. "What was that?" I exclaimed as I stepped back. Sue laughed, "You've seen your first gar fish." I pulled myself away from the water and my new friend. Time had slipped away as fast as the flowing current. Heading back to the house, I realized I felt lighter. Florida was full of surprises.

LITTLE WEKIVA MEMORIES

Spurred on by my experience with Sue, I started reading about Florida's springs. These sparkling jewels dot the landscape. The clear waters of the springs found near our home along the Wekiva River in Seminole County boil up from the aquifers at a refreshing 72—76 degrees. Most spring water throughout the state ranges between 64-86 degrees.

Leif and I discovered that the river and springs are constantly evolving. If you pay attention, you'll notice subtle changes as the banks recede and widen. Shallows and valleys form underwater. Hollows along the shore hint at nighttime resting spots for animals—alligators, maybe large snakes, perhaps otters. This is their habitat; we are just sharing it.

The next time I spotted my neighbor by the water, I headed right out to greet her. Sue's easy manner and good humor set me at ease which I had not felt since we had moved to Florida. It felt good to relax by the water. I was intrigued by the newness of this experience and the many different things to discover by the water's edge. Much of what surrounded me in Florida still made me uncomfortable. Sue, on the other hand, was completely at home in her surroundings. She expressed her love for Florida in ways that were giving me a great counterpoint to the things that I found disconcerting. Sue would turn her face upward and smile. She reveled in the heat, soaking up the sun's rays, letting the warmth radiate all the way to her bones. The sounds that were unnerving to me, were for Sue, simply conversations from creatures sharing her space. The buzzing, hissing, and clicks all told tales of creatures going about their business. Sue was a natural at telling stories about Florida wildlife, weaving them into our conversations. Her beloved Florida was opening its arms to me.

It did not take me long to start joining Sue in the river. I'd often grab a heavy rake and give her a hand clearing debris. The babbling water gossiped about life further up the river. What was lost, we found. The occasional baseball or frisbee floated by. Beer cans, with brands no longer sold, showed up in tangles of wood trapped around the posts of our bridge. We dug bottles out of the sand. Leif discovered fossilized shark teeth hidden in the sandy bottom. There was a thrill that came with discovery of things long submerged.

Mr. Oliver's treehouse bridge

While working in the river together, I came to learn that Sue and Mr. Oliver, who owned the property next to us, were good friends and colleagues. Sue and her dogs often kept Mr. O and his dog, Wolfie, company. She would hop on her golf cart and drive over from her home a few blocks away to Mr. O's octagon-shaped home nestled in the woods a few hundred feet from the river. He added boardwalks and gazebos by the water's edge. Sue and Mr. O enjoyed sitting together in the gazebo, watching as evening slipped in and the alligators surfaced.

Mr. O and Sue jointly owned an interesting business venture together. The company was a major supplier of rigging in the greater Orlando area. Their complex woven lines of rope were used by shipping companies, builders, and even Disney World. Mr. O used this creative ingenuity to build a drawbridge over the river that ran through his property. The bridge supported a treehouse structure perched high above the water. The kids and I were invited to explore which was great fun! Heavy rigging helped us navigate planks that carried us to each level of the treehouse. Each lookout provided a unique vantage point of the river. This birds eye view gave us a beautiful sight line, changing our perspective. As is often the case, when we look at things from a different angle, our appreciation grows because we see things we missed before. I had been learning to love the little things about my surroundings—the things I was studying up close. With each magical step on the swinging bridge to the tree tops, my point of view expanded. I discovered new marvels. Further down the river, a little pool formed. Dark shadows obscuring the river bottom made me wonder what creatures lurked there. Hawks floated by, giving me the eye. I noticed a boardwalk that disappeared in the woods. Sue told me that bears used the walkway to forage for berries that grew in the thickets nearby. On the way back to the ground, we laughed as Sue pointed out the bear scat in the corner of one of the landings. It was funny to imagine bears navigating the precarious drawbridge to check out the same view we were enjoying. Somehow, thinking of a bear in a tree house made me feel less frightened about a bear in my backyard. It brought me a sense of joy as I realized my frame of mind was changing. Florida was continuing to surprise me.

A birds eye view

Bear helping himself to oranges

I started running a tally of the bears we saw in the yard. I was amazed when the head count quickly reached ten. Big papa bears and protective mamas with cute cubs stopped by on a regular basis. Frequently I would look up from yard work to see a bear ambling by or a deer staring me down. One morning, two big bears boldly strolled through the back yard, slowing lumbering across our bridge. They took their time, nudging each other gently, and then stood on hind legs, going paw to paw, leaning in, pushing back and collapsing into a roll as if playing on an imaginary hamster wheel.

One evening, when Jeff got home from work, I couldn't wait to tell him about the latest bear encounter! "He was as big as you!" I exclaimed. Jeff wasn't impressed with the implication of that comparison. I went on to explain my encounter, how I had burst into the garage, quickly pulling up short when, not six feet in front of me, I saw the biggest bear I have ever seen. He had his head buried in a garbage bag. The bear was plainly annoyed at me for rudely interrupting his dinner. He raised his head, shook it from side to side, made a snort of as if to say, "Oh bother." Then he thrust his head back into the bag, deciding I wasn't much of a threat to him or his meal. That big bear was between me and my car. I quickly pieced together what had happened. Our son, new to the driving routine, was having a hard time remembering to close the garage door when he left in the morning. Florida 101: You do not leave your garage door open! Snakes, salamanders, lizards, spiders, and . . . bears come right on in! I backed into the house. Collecting my thoughts, I reopened the door a crack, slid my arm through that crack, and reached stealthily for the garage door button. The rattle gave the big boy a bit of a start. He stomped out into the sunlight, but then came back for his sack lunch. Dragging the garbage bag with him to the driveway, he proceeded to carry on with his dinner. Just another example of "normal" in Florida.

In our early years in Florida, as I tried to make peace with all that was unfamiliar to me, animal encounters became less scary and more adventuresome. Bear sightings grew to be well over 100. Even though I've long ago stopped counting, it's still exciting every time we see them. Snakes, on the other hand, like to hide, so we don't see them that often. Once in a while they'll show up along the riverbank, coiled in the sun. Sometimes they slink across the front walk or slither through the grass. I wouldn't say I'm comfortable with snakes, but I have learned to appreciate them for their helpfulness. They eat rodents! When I see them now, I'll pause, look for identifying marks—"Red on Yellow, Kill a Fellow, Red on Black, Friend of Jack," and let them carry on their way, thankful because I don't have mice in my attic.

Seeing the joy our young son had for all the creatures he found in our yard also softened my heart toward Florida. One day, when we were outside playing, Leif was collecting frogs and digging for worms when he shouted, "Look!" We all stopped and turned toward him. In one hand, he held a frog, its head peaking out of his little fist and legs dangling out the other side. His other hand held a worm that wobbled as Leif pointed toward the trees. Our eyes searched the leafy branches. Clinging to the tree trunk was a mommy bear and her two cubs. Life was grand! Just another afternoon in Florida.

Bobcat seen near south run of Sanlando Spring (Dean Mickelson)

The kids and I were beginning to love our afternoons playing in the sunshine, chasing lizards, collecting frogs, catching fish, counting bears, and splashing in the water. We felt like the previously accepted order of human and nature interaction was off balance. The reversals we were experiencing felt like a wrong was being set right. We were the caged animals, safely tucked in our screened-in porch with the bears watching us from their natural habitat in the trees instead of behind bars in a zoo.

The wonder of watching animals in their environment never grows old. One day, I passed through the room where our piano tuner was plucking and plunking away when, out of the corner of my eye, I caught a glimpse of a shape that stood out on the creek bank. The two of us peered out the window. With the help of binoculars, we got a good look at a big alligator. He had climbed up out of the river and seemed to be enjoying the sunshine. Another day, we were excited to see a bobcat stealthily tracking something across the yard. A few days later, he showed up again. We watched as he scampered across our bridge, nose in the air, ears pointed, ever aware of what was going on around him. These animal encounters have become a treasured gift!

After several years of help from Guillermo, we were finally able to keep the bugs outside. I still do not like cockroaches, but I can deal with the occasional bug. I've learned what I need to be careful about and what is not a big deal. Those banana spiders are extremely venomous, but its venom is not potent enough to kill a human. Nonetheless, a bite from a banana spider will cause painful blisters. Red ants also have a nasty bite, but we've learned how to avoid, how to protect,

OUR STORY

and how to heal. We have also learned that it's silly worrying about alligators hiding out under cars. That is a highly unlikely scenario! Those gators mind their own business; if we leave them alone, they'll leave us alone. As far as the bears are concerned, we are totally uninteresting. A few tips we learned on coexisting with bears: Do not bother them or feed them, keep away from mama bears and their cubs, and remember to close garage doors and secure garbage can lids.

My focus has changed. I revel in the unusual beauty of Florida. I have come to cherish the citrus that pops up on trees in our yard. From Mid-November through January, we can walk outside and pick juicy lemons and large grapefruit. The sweet, delicate scent of orange blossoms hangs in the air. In January, gorgeous camellias bud. Their blossoms are heavy on the bush, causing branches to bend. When February wind chill and blizzards blast in Minnesota and other parts of the country, we are enjoying "crisp" 65-degree mornings that unfold into 75-degree days highlighted with blue skies and sunshine. The loons from the North come here in the winter. They know instinctively what I've learned. Florida is special.

Camelia

OUR STORY

Orange Blossom

23

I found myself telling people that our house came with the creek. That beautiful creek, lazily threading its way through the brush and trees at the back edge of our property, was softening my heart. I now treasure time spent on its banks. In the quiet, white egrets balance on spindly legs. Otters and their babies splash in the water. I've grown to admire the palm trees scattered among the cypress near the water.

"Who needs therapy when you have the creek to play in." Sue's words often ring in my ear. A few years ago, she sold her home next to us after Mr. O had passed away. Sue had been a devoted caregiver as he battled cancer. It all happened quickly. Before I even knew he was sick, he was gone. Sitting on the decking that Mr. Oliver had built near the waters edge, Sue's story unfolded. The woman that we came to know as a partner and friend to Mr O had actually been married to him for 10 years. Sue explained that the marriage was something special between the two of them. Their secret kept the relationship spicy. It seemed very much the kind of thing Sue would do. My free-spirited friend, who loved playing in the creek in her nude bathing suit, would certainly be the kind of woman that would cherish a sweet, private romance.

LITTLE WEKIVA MEMORIES

Sue was busy finding a good buyer for their business and their home by the creek. She was sad, yet practical about the situation, recognizing that life is lived in chapters. In the next phase of her life, she'd be enjoying ocean sunsets from her beach condo. Our time together changed. She would swing into our drive on her golf cart and we'd walk together down to the water's edge, both of us in shorts and flip flops. Our conversations would ebb and flow with the river. We'd talk about the bald eagle dipping into the yard for lunch, or the fresh water ray that Leif and I saw on our recent kayak trip to the spring. We'd talk about our families and share, as friends do, the things that make us sad and things that bring us joy. I always felt better, more grounded, after spending time with Sue. As we sat by the creek, nature's noises eased into a restful hum. We enjoyed the quiet, together.

Sometimes I'd ride my bike over to Sue's place, a few streets away. She'd welcome me into the courtyard of her home. A frond-covered tiki bar made the pool area feel like a whimsical garden with bright yellow, wrought iron daisy benches and little wooden bridges crisscrossing the garden area. I plopped myself down in a blue wicker swing for a rest. Sue had been spending a lot of time with her aging parents. This and the other recent changes in her life had been difficult, but she was matter-of-fact and good-humored about it all. She missed her regular "therapy" time in the creek. I assured her, again, that she could come over anytime she needed to clear her head. Pointing to a ladder propped up against the back of her house she said, "Sometimes I climb onto the roof and watch the stars. Just like I used to do with Mr. O down by the river." Sue turned to me and said, "Thanks for being in my life." Her words were unexpected. I felt so grateful that she was in *my* life. Sue had opened my eyes to a new world and softened its hard edges. She encouraged me to notice the beauty hidden all around me. She taught me how to appreciate the simple pleasures of my surroundings. Sue helped me learn how to live in Florida.

LITTLE WEKIVA MEMORIES

Our family has been in Florida for fifteen years now. Sue has since moved to her condo on the beach where she enjoys glorious sunrises and salty air. I miss her. She gave Leif and me a wonderful gift—opening our eyes to the wonders of Florida. My family and I now spend a lot of time down by the creek. We invite friends to play there with us. The driftwood we pull from the creek fuels fires for roasting hot dogs and s'mores. The fast moving water gives the kids a challenge as they balance on paddle boards or navigate with their canoe. Standing in the creek, with our feet sinking into the sandy bottom, we revel in the coolness of the water. We're in tune with the rhythm of the river now. By November, nature's supercharged speed of growth slows. Vines die back, and the creek is more navigable without the encroaching plant life. In February, tiny hints of green tinge the trees. New growth forms in March and April. By May, and all the way through October, the woods will again be dense, harboring mysteries in the creeping cover.

Recently, we were down by the creek with friends who were visiting from up north. Jeff had made a small fire from branches he cleared from the woods. The coals were ideal for roasting marshmallows. It wasn't long before the kids were playing in the water and jumping from our bridge onto inner tubes in the river, then floating down towards Mr. O's landmark bridge. I turned, from watching them fight the current back up stream, to look at the beautiful spot where the river angles sharply.

I was amazed at the seemingly endless varieties of plant life. The green leaves come in so many different shapes. Long skinny leaves with sharp edges. Short, dark and shiny ones. Some are round, broad and wavy, with fan-like fronds. One palm tree I noticed had fronds that could cover the hood of my car. There are tiny, mouse ear sized leaves and leaves shaped like elephant ears. The colors range from deep green, frosty gray-green to green tinged with yellow.

The clouds were like cotton balls, ones that have been stretched loosely across the blue sky. The sight reminded me of Georgia O'Keeffe's painting *Sky Above the Clouds*.

OUR STORY

    A few months later, I returned to Florida after visiting our daughter in the frigid mid-west where wind gusts carrying 7-degree temperatures sucked the air out of me. Landing at the airport and hopping the tram to the terminal, I laughed to myself as I listened to the now familiar, pre-recorded message from Orlando mayor, Buddy Dyer: "Whether you're visiting, or you call Florida home, welcome to the city beautiful." I looked out at the palm trees standing tall in the blinding sun and realized that yes, I called this home. A smile spread across my face as I gazed at those puffy, fluffy, sun-kissed clouds.
    Driving into our neighborhood, I felt a welcoming embrace from the outstretched branches of those grand Southern live oaks. I looked out at the hood of my car and what should I see looking back at me? The bulging eyes of a lizard, clinging to the hood. Just another day in Florida!

ADVENTURES ON THE LITTLE WEKIVA RIVER
DISCOVERING THE SPRINGS

Sanlando, Palm, Starbuck, Ginger Ale, and Pegasus—Leif

Introduction

To fully understand the story of Florida's springs, we must consider the first caretakers of Florida. *Seminole History* explains that, in the 1770s, diverse groups of Native Americans living throughout Florida "collectively became known as Seminoles."[1] From the mid-18th century to the mid-19th century, Native Americans living along the rivers and in the forests of Florida, resisted colonization and development, calling themselves the "Unconquered People." These Seminole Indians fought for their home in Florida as more and more Native American groups were being pushed south by white settlers.

The five springs along the Little Wekiva River were no doubt intimately known by native tribes who revered nature. These ideas led to a spiritual relationship with the land, waterways and springs. I imagine homes with cooking fires burning along the shore, children playing in the shallows, and hunting parties patrolling the spring pools. Seminoles used weapons like spears and bows to hunt local wildlife—longtime residents tell stories of finding arrowheads in swampy thickets.

Unfortunately, a series of conflicts and wars led to the scattering of the Seminole people. The vast majority was forced to Oklahoma on the Trail of Tears while a small group of about 200 retreated deep into the Everglades. Florida's wilderness was left untended, and signs of human presence disappeared.

Slowly, as Northerners trickled into the area lured by tales of opportunity, the land reawakened. To these new settlers, Florida was an uncharted land of promise. The stories and histories I share here highlight those settlers as they strove to tame the wilderness, make ends meet, and rediscover the springs that were known so intimately by native tribes. My stories bring into focus the perspective of someone who enjoys life along the Little Wekiva River today.

Sanlando Springs

The sights and sounds of the creek met Max, Juliet, and me as we set out on the river. Every week or so, we would pull down the long, orange kayaks from their makeshift stands under the grapefruit tree, drag them across the wet grass, and plunge them headfirst into the river. The remains of a concrete bridge have settled into the stream, providing a launch for our boats.

Old pictures that our neighbor, Sue, has shared with us suggest that it was once covered in grass and spanned what was then Starbuck Springs Run. Sue remembers that "A hurricane, or maybe tropical storm Fay, flooded the spring and river, felled trees, and changed the flow drastically. Best I can remember, the river changed after a hurricane, then again after Crane's Roost [was built near Downtown Altamonte]." The river has now merged with Starbuck Run, drowning the concrete bridge in the process.

My brother, Max, began propelling us forward. Juliet, my sister, paddled ahead and circled back towards us as we passed the crystal clear stream of water flowing from the spring. After a tricky turn past an eddy, we pushed further upstream where the overhanging foliage left sun-dappled patterns on the water.

"Here's the swing!" Juliet called over her shoulder.

Sure enough, the green disc swing hung lazily over a deep pool. About a quarter mile upriver from our house, that swing served as a waypoint. We often stopped there to play for a bit. Continuing along the Little Wekiva, we enjoyed the changes that each twist and turn brought. Every section of the river seemed different. Past the rope swing, rustling trees and vines shaded broad shallows. We could reach out with our fingers and brush the sandy bottom. Further along, the shallows gave way to a deeper channel. The trees shrunk away, leaving the sun to glare down upon the swift flowing creek. Swamp grass and kudzu cloaked the banks and trees, forming strange shapes and shadows.

We forged past a section of the river where homes on Markham Woods Road have creek access. Private boardwalks lead to cleared areas on the riverbank, where small clusters of gazebos and benches overlook the stream. Although we kayaked the river often, we always noticed something new. That Saturday, I glimpsed another rope swing tucked behind a tree. I imagined how fun it would be to swing over the deep spot in the middle of the stream, and just let go.

"A stop for next time," I remarked.

As we neared our destination, the river tightened, and cypress roots swayed in the water beneath us.

"There's the first bridge!" I remarked, pointing overhead. "Four more to go."

As we cruised forward and gazed upwards, the rusted bulk of an arched bridge drifted past. Through the years, we'd memorized where the five bridges were within the half mile upriver from our house. After the next bridge, we spotted a weir off to the left with water pouring over the rim that carved a deep pool in the riverside where we pulled in our kayaks.

Sanlando Springs entering the Little Wekiva river

"Let's stop here. I've never been up to see what's behind this waterfall," I said as I lugged the kayak toward the bank and scrambled to the side. Normally, we continued upriver until we arrived at the second weir. There, the cold, clear waters of Sanlando Springs met the dark, tannic Little Wekiva for the first time. The line between them was striking. We always stopped by the little waterfall spilling over the weir and played in the swirling pool beneath it. Sometimes we walked through a small stand of pine trees to this beautiful spot by the creek. Today was different—I wanted to see where the second weir led me.

I grabbed the rope attached to the kayak's bow and looped it round a cypress knob. It was only a quick scramble up the bank before I arrived at the top of the concrete weir. Behind me was the Little Wekiva and the spring water rushing into it. In front of me was a pond covered in lily-pads, stretching beyond where I could see. I chose my way carefully along the bank, following the path of slow moving water. As I rounded the bend, I saw a more complete picture of the waterway. "*This must be Sanlando Springs Run,*" I thought to myself. Sure enough, on my right, I saw the 'pond's' source—Sanlando Springs. The clear water of the spring spilled through the hole in yet another weir.

*Sanlando vintage, 1930s
(Overstreet Family)*

Surveying the well-manicured area around the water, I was amazed at how big the spring stretching out before me was. Sanlando is the largest of the five springs on the Little Wekiva River, and the spring most often visited by people who live in The Springs Community.

As described in the "Sanlando Springs" entry on the St. Johns River Water Management District (SJRWMD) website, "Sanlando is a second magnitude spring that flows mostly from an oblong cavity beneath a limestone ledge about 7 feet below the water surface [that is] . . . 2 to 3 feet high and 10 feet wide."[2] The spring pool is 200 by 180 feet wide.

The dark-teal waters of the spring are separated from the sloping lawn by a concrete retention wall and sidewalk that allows bathers to slip into the shallow water on one end or take a brave plunge directly over the spring boil. A white sand beach stretches along the opposite side where people enjoy sitting by the sparkling water. Two gates allow water to exit the spring pool on either end, flowing through a series of ponds and streams before plunging into the Little Wekiva through two weirs. The

structure and layout of the spring area has remained largely the same since the mid 1920s, except for the removal of a slide and diving board.

People still lounge by the shore. A raft bobs playfully in the middle of the spring. You can hear the thwacks of the tennis rackets from the nearby court, although those are now accompanied by pickle ball dinks and slams. On the weekends, you'll find kids playing on the basketball courts or walking on the nearby boardwalk. Residents of The Springs continue to enjoy the area as people have done for generations.

In some ways, the spring and people's enjoyment of it hasn't changed. In other ways, compared to what it once was, Sanlando Springs is drastically different. The story that follows highlights these changes.

The story begins in the mid-1800s with Ingram Fletcher. The prominent Indianapolis banker and his brother, Albert, followed in the footsteps of their father who started what would become the Fletcher & Sharpe Bank. After their father's death, the brothers joined forces with Thomas Sharpe and continued the family business. The people of Indianapolis trusted the well-established bank, so Ingram, Albert, and Thomas quickly developed significant wealth and influence. "The Fall of the House of Fletcher" explains that, "Although Indianapolis was struggling with a financial depression in the 1870's, business was booming at the Fletcher & Sharpe Bank."[3] This allowed Albert and his wife to build an extravagant home in downtown Indianapolis.

Both Albert and Ingram Fletcher were on top of the world. Soon, however, a shocking blow ended the opulent life enjoyed by the Fletcher family. "On the morning of July 15, 1884, customers arrived at the Fletcher & Sharpe bank to find [a] notice posted on the door."[3] The bank had decided to suspend payments due to crippling debt. Inevitably, a combination of passive business strategies and general economic hardship had taken its toll on the most trusted bank in town. After the crash, Ingram and his brother were both forced to sell nearly all of their personal property in an effort to keep the business afloat. Alas, their attempts came up short by $600,000. Albert, having fallen from grace, took a job in sales and made several moves before dying in 1918. Ingram, however, decided to start a new life in a land filled with possibility: Florida.

Ingram and his wife, Gertrude, decided to settle near her parents in central Florida. They purchased 161 acres with the intention of creating a new railroad hub. The property was located at the intersection of two major railroads where today Interstate 4 and State Road 434 intersect. The land was also positioned in a watershed that featured several springs. He began to work feverishly on plans for a new settlement by the railroad with hopes of regaining his prior wealth and success. The Fletchers dubbed the largest spring on their property Hoosier Springs (present day Sanlando Springs), in remembrance of the nickname of their home state, Indiana. "The land itself [was] subdivided in 1885 as both a personal residence on the Wekiva River and a town of 'Hoosier Springs' on the south side of the planned Florida Midland Railway track."[4] Unfortunately,

Ingram Fletcher family (historicindianapolis.com)

Ingram's fledgling town never flourished due to his inability to sell most of the town plots; however, the name still clung to local landmarks such as the Hoosier Springs Orange Grove. The Fletchers sold their township in 1887, but they maintained a presence in the community.

The Fletchers tried their hand at several trades including opening a little bookstore. Life began to improve for the couple once again. Then, "In 1891, President Benjamin Harrison commissioned (Ingram) as Orlando's postmaster. He later became the first cashier of the State Bank of Orlando."³ For many during the late Gilded Age, Florida was a land of beauty, healing, and opportunity. Although the Indiana banker hit rock bottom in his home state, he was soon able to make a life for himself in his adopted state. Like many others, he was intoxicated with the charm and tranquility of this wild land.

The next chapter in the story of Sanlando Springs features Elizabeth McClain Saunders. In the late 1880s, she and her two sons made the 1,268 mile journey from Toronto, Canada, to what is now Longwood, Florida. While Ingram Fletcher traveled here with hopes of a new life, Elizabeth traveled with hopes of health and happiness for one of her sons who was struggling with an illness. People of that era viewed the humid, warm climate as a kind of cure-all for sickness. Americans also revered spring bathing as the ultimate therapeutic activity. Victorian Age spas often centered around natural springs and advertised cures for any conceivable illness. Two of the most popular locations were in Saratoga Springs, New York, and Warm Springs, Georgia (the latter made famous by Franklin Delano Roosevelt, who visited often to relieve pain caused by polio). The Victorian interest in spring bathing has been validated by modern scientific knowledge which shows that these natural water sources contain important healing minerals such as calcium and magnesium.

Elizabeth Saunders (blogspot.com)

"Spa Culture" was nothing new. Even before Europeans embraced the benefits of spring water, many Native American tribes had a strong spiritual reverence for springs. Victorian culture borrowed from those ideas and the long history of spring bathing in Europe. For years, those activities were inaccessible for the working class because they couldn't

FDR at Warm Springs, GA 1928 (Wikipedia)

Hoosier Springs, 1888 (State Library and Archives of Florida)

afford to travel to the places where springs were found. As explained in Rick Kilby's *Florida's Healing Waters*, "Initially only the wealthy escaped the increasingly polluted and disease-plagued cities for spas in the country. But as trains made travel more affordable, people with lesser means could seek health from the nation's mineral springs."[5]

Undoubtably, the Saunders family immigrated south to experience the healing waters of Florida. Like the Fletchers, they were enticed by the string of crystalline springs along the Little Wekiva. After purchasing Ingram's failed settlement in 1887, Elizabeth immediately began making herself and her two sons comfortable in their new home. Mr. Saunders had passed away years earlier, leaving Elizabeth a widow—albeit a financially secure one. She had taken the reins of both bread-winning and child-rearing after his death in an unconventional and impressive move for the time. The Saunders family settled into a home near Hoosier Springs as Elizabeth began planning a town plat bigger and better than the abandoned Fletcher project. She realized the strategic location of her property and sought to do what her predecessors could not. Immediately, she set to work creating a new community: Palm Springs. Elizabeth's settlement was named after a smaller sulfur spring nearby rather than the central Hoosier Spring.

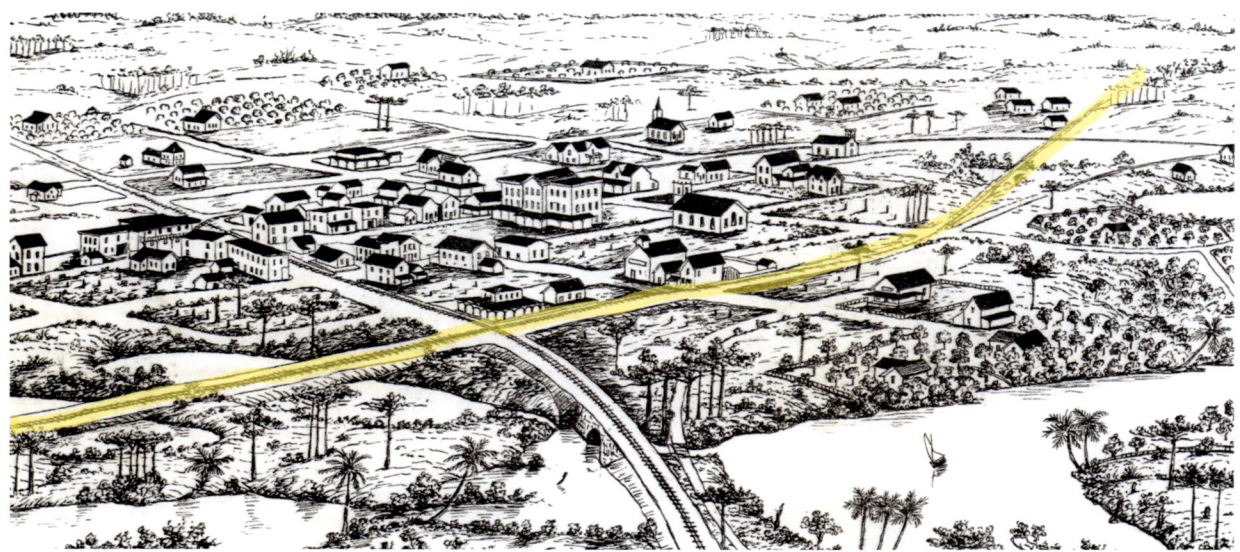

Photo of Early railroad intersection near 434 and Markham Woods Rd. (Historiclongwood.com)

The widowed Saunders had two things working in her favor. As stated previously, "The *Orange Belt Railway* and *Florida Midland Railway* crossed where today State Road 434 meets Markham Woods Road."[6] The preexisting crossroad allowed an easy way for prospective land buyers from the north to get around. Elizabeth also had two foundations on which to build her town. Just south of Hoosier was another small town known as Altamont, which was "first envisioned in 1874 by a successful New York doctor, Washington Kilmer."[6] Despite his medical prowess, he too was susceptible to the pitfalls of failed pioneering. Altamont did not take off at the time any more than Hoosier Springs did. Although the town itself failed, its legacy, like that of Hoosier Springs, has lived on. For example, the city of Altamonte—with an "e"—exists very near to the spot on which Kilmer's settlement was located. After turning over his land to Ms. Saunders, Kilmer returned to the field of education and medicine.

Saunders, with the unused town plats of both Hoosier Springs and Altamont, was able to draw up a new city plan. Her settlement, Palm Springs, was centered around the railroad intersection that extended north beyond what is now Interstate 4, and south, deeper into current-day Longwood. Her community also encompassed much of what is, today, The Springs neighborhood. Saunders poured her heart and soul into the town of Palm Springs. She worked to reconfigure the plats laid out by Kilmer and Fletcher and soon decided to implement "town squares" to break up the monotony of lot after lot. Her town was nestled between huge orange groves and two major railways, suggesting inevitable success; however, just as her predecessors had, she struggled to make a success of her venture. Palm Springs was never a very successful town. Most likely, nearby settlements made it difficult for a new one to flourish. However, unlike Ingram Fletcher, she was able to sell a few plots of her planned community to a handful of prospective buyers. One of those buyers was William Massey, the man that would soon become Elizabeth's second husband. After the sale of a few more of her plots, the town of Palm Springs was, "Complete with not-one-but-two railroads, a post office, and several stores, it had a population of over 300 by 1890."[7] Still, her settlement was small and short-lived compared to neighboring towns. Her new husband, William, was short-lived as well; Widow Saunders soon became Widow Massey.

Elizabeth lost "two husbands and five of her children prior to 1900. The son she brought south because of his poor health, John McClain Saunders, was buried at Greenwood Cemetery in Orlando after his death, August 30, 1906."[4] Elizabeth returned to her home in Canada. Life was obviously difficult for any early settler, let alone a woman. It was almost unheard of for a widowed woman to have any social or economic relevance at the time. Although Ms. Saunders-Massey never made a great success of her community, she did leave a mark as an Orange County pioneer that overcame all odds and provided for her dwindling family.

After the early attempts by Fletcher and Saunders-Massey to develop the area around Hoosier Springs, other landowners made their mark. Through the years, the property surrounding the springs has changed hands several times, but the springs continue to intrigue people with their gifts of beauty, healing properties and the sense of community that they inspire.

And here I was, over 100 years later, still appreciating that gift. I pulled myself away from the beauty before me and began retracing my steps along the lily-covered run when I noticed a massive snapping turtle drifting through the water, its back covered in swaying algae. As I approached the weir once more, I heard Max and Juliet's voices mingle with the rush of water. Jumping in my kayak again, we were off. There was always something more to discover in the springs.

ADVENTURES ON THE LITTLE WEKIVA RIVER

Sanlando Springs

Palm Springs

Bonfires and S'mores. Hotdogs. Kayaking. If I'm having friends over, we usually end up at the creek. When we take off on our journeys, sometimes we'll see other people on the Little Wekiva.

For the most part, the river is empty, quiet, and secluded. Occasionally we will pass another explorer. The cast of characters ranges from young adults, the stereotypical "Florida Man," kayakers from in and around The Springs neighborhood, and a handful of shark tooth hunters. Yes, shark teeth can be found throughout the Little Wekiva River, as they can in many other Florida waterways. At first, we were confused by "prospectors" panning for who knows what in the river. Ziplock bags holding little black specks were stashed carefully in their backpacks.

ADVENTURES ON THE LITTLE WEKIVA RIVER

Friends at creek

47

Eventually we asked what they were searching for. "Shark teeth," they said. "They're small, but you can find a lot of them if you look." I was excited about the possibility of another place to hunt for treasure. I'm an avid collector of many things, ranging from rocks and shells to sea glass and bones. In fact, I even had a pre-existing shark tooth collection from trips to the ocean. When I began searching for the teeth in the river, I looked almost exclusively at the entrance of Sanlando Springs Run. I found small but plentiful specimens. Later I looked and found shark teeth in other places along the river, including by our house.

water comes aquatic, amphibious, and reptilian creatures of the past. Besides modern shark teeth, their predecessors megalodon, glyptodont, mastodon, mammoth, giant sloth, whale, alligator, camel, and saber-toothed cat fossils can also be found.

Shell plating *Picture of Holmesia (dinopedia.org)*

Shark teeth collection

The river holds other secrets as well. I had never associated fossil hunting with Florida. When I thought about it, however, it made sense. Sandbars such as Florida were once covered with water. With

The revelation of Floridian paleontology was another surprise for our family. I remember the first summer I went to camp in Florida. There was a display of gargantuan mammoth bones dredged from the camp's swimming hole. *"Why don't they have these in the Smithsonian?"* I wondered. I soon learned that it was not uncommon to find fossils like this in Florida. One of my favorite finds on the river was the shell-plating of an ancient armadillo-like creature: a holmesina. Although similar to their modern day counterparts, these armadillos were much larger, around the size and weight of a Volkswagen Beetle.

Another spot where I often looked for shark teeth was Palm Springs—a midsize spring within easy wading distance of Sanlando. You can always smell the spring before you can see it. Sulfur odors from the boil make everything smell a bit eggy. The next giveaways are the straggly white root clusters, coated in sulfur bacteria in the spring water. The effect of the sulfur is evident in the spring pool as well. Crayfish and minnows, all bleached white, swim in the area. The SJRWMD entry "Palm Springs" describes it as a "third-magnitude spring enclosed by a 4-foot high concrete retaining wall that once formed a swimming pool. The pool is about 100 feet long and 50 feet wide. Spring discharge was from under a rock ledge in a circular vent near the southwest edge of the pool."[8] The retaining wall has a gap that allows kayaks to slide into the main pool, and the vent is just deep enough for a safe cannonball into the spring. Although lily-pads cover the spring run, as well as the entrance to the main pool, the surface of the spring itself is clear and the water, cool.

Palm Springs boil

Citrus freeze (State Library and Archives of Florida)

    Like the other springs on the Little Wekiva River, the history of Palm Springs is closely tied to the history of Sanlando Springs (then Hoosier).

    After Saunder-Massey's attempt at development, the area around Hoosier Springs seemed doomed. The failure of these settlements was likely due to competition with other nearby towns. This was undoubtably compounded by several cold winters that caused economic hardship within the developing citrus industry. Freezing temperatures in Florida during the winters of 1894, 1895, and "another in 1899 put many north-central and northeast Florida producers out of business."[9] Because of this, the intersection of the Florida Midland and Orange Belt Railroads, crossing right near Palm Springs, was no longer a busy railroad hub, therefore the town was not as desirable.

    The story of Palm Springs took another interesting turn as the Beeman family, whose claim to fame was chewing gum, moved to Central Florida. Dr. Edward Beeman was a great titan of 19th century American commerce. Chewing gum was rising in popularity, and Dr. Beeman was inspired to add his pepsin powder, a digestive aid, to the gum currently on the market. "Most gum on the market didn't taste too great, and they lost their flavor after a very short time. They also didn't serve any greater purpose, beyond just exercising your jaw bone."⁷ The unsavory flavor of the gum was due to chicle: a substance used to add elasticity. By adding pepsin powder, Beeman was able to mask the flavor of chicle. His invention exploded. With the financial windfall from gum, Beeman wintered in Florida with his family. Dr. Beeman's son's, Harry and Lester, both settled in Florida in the late 1880s. They immersed themselves in the state's growing industries: citrus, ranching, and real estate.

One of Lester's investments in the mid-1910s was a recreational area 20 minutes north of the city of Orlando, called Palm Spring. Lester purchased a large portion of Elizabeth Saunder-Massey's former property that included Palm Springs, and a few other mineral springs nearby. Hoosier Springs was notably absent from his plot. He enclosed the largest spring on his property, Palm Springs, with a concrete retaining wall, converting it into a recreational pool complete with a bathhouse. Over time, Beeman further developed the area and promoted the spring as a swimming spot.

Palm Springs operated independently for several years. In 1925 Lester sold the Palm Springs property. A few years later, following his father's death, Beeman decided he still loved Palm Springs and bought it back. He continued to develop and utilize his property throughout the 1930s, but competition from next door soon made economic success difficult.⁷

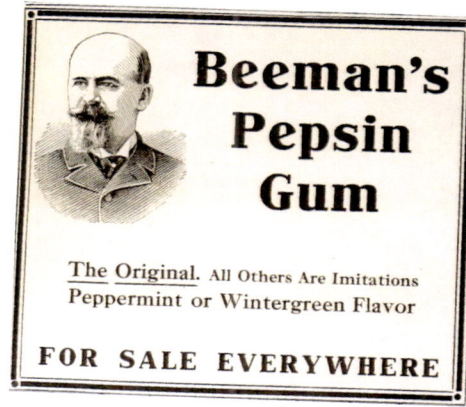

Beeman gum (eBay.com)

Ladies splashing in the cool waters of Palm Springs, late 1920s (Overstreet Family)

That competition began with James Franklin Haithcox, "a minor stage actor turned salesman who opened his own real-estate company in Orlando in the mid-1920s."[10] Haithcox became a major land developer who helped chart the path of Central Florida. He had acquired land around the springs in the early 1920s, save for the plot owned by the Beemans. In 1925, the Moses Overstreet Investment Company, which now owned the property around Hoosier Spring, leased the spring itself to Haithcox. Shortly after, he began developing the area into a lucrative tourist attraction. "At the springs, Haithcox built a dam to raise the water level, landscaped the shoreline with tropical plants and added a swimming pool and bathhouse."[10] The Olympic size swimming pool was filled with actual spring water. The dam built by Haithcox was especially significant because, prior to development, river water mixed with the spring water in low lying areas. By contrast, Palm Springs' well-defined boundary had made it the more popular swimming spot before Haithcox's changes at the now renamed Sanlando Spring.

Pool at Sanlando Springs in the 1920s (State Library and Archives of Florida)

Renaming Hoosier Springs "Sanlando Springs" mirrored its geographic position between the growing cities of Sanford and Orlando. The name change was also rooted in a desire to claim Hoosier as his own; Sanlando was a trademark that identified Haithcox as the developer. He also established the surrounding area as "Sanlando Springs Tropical Park" in 1925. Sanlando Springs remained a popular tourist destination throughout the 1920s, but Moses Overstreet repossessed Sanlando Springs Tropical Park when Haithcox was forced into foreclosure.[11]

The Great Depression forced Frank Haithcox to relinquish his property, but this was not the end of the story for the park. Robert "Bob" Overstreet, Moses's son, believed in the success of Sanlando Tropical Park. He invested time and significant money, revitalizing the popular playground. One of the most significant additions was the planting of 10,000 azalea bushes in preparation for the park's reopening.

Sanlando Springs entrance sign 1924 (State Library and Archives of Florida)

Sanlando Springs early years 1920s (State Library and Archives of Florida)

*Old Sanlando photo with sign 1940s.
(State Library and Archives of Florida)*

"The park also offered swimming lessons and weekly aquatic shows. The Marchand family, extremely famous at the time for their log rolling skills, put on professional demonstrations at the spring. After dark, the pavilion at Sanlando Springs opened for dances that drew many young people in the 1940s."[12] Despite changes in ownership, Sanlando Springs Tropical Park continued to draw crowds throughout the mid 20th century.

In 1935, around the time of Overstreet's reopening, Lester Beeman was forced to sell his beloved Palm Springs property once and for all. A combination of economic factors and Overstreet's tough competition made ownership of his plot unrealistic. Nine years later, "In 1944, Mr. Overstreet purchased Palm Springs with plans to add it to Sanlando Tropical Park."[13] Finally, after many years of separate ownership, Sanlando and Palm Springs were under the same management.

The park, with the two iconic springs, was a favorite getaway for locals looking to relax. Floridians seeking relief from the sweltering heat found it in the cool, clear waters of the springs.

Palm Springs has since fallen into disrepair. The entire left side of the wall is slanted towards the water and partially collapsed. The site stands as a stark contrast to well-maintained Sanlando Springs, but visitors still enjoy the clear water and the memories the place brings to mind.

One of our recent visits to Palm Springs stands out in my mind. Mom, Dad, and I were traveling upriver in our kayaks for a relaxing afternoon paddle. It was a cool day. The sun was shining on the water.

"Make sure to back paddle around that corner," Mom remarked. The river made a sharp turn up ahead, and Dad and I were aimed directly towards the opposite shoreline. A bramble of foliage and overhanging branches extended over the water. We both leaned to our left and dug our paddles into the water, trying to reposition our craft to face upriver. The bow of the kayak began to turn slightly in the right direction, so we let up.

"We need more!" shouted Dad.

The sharp turn of the creek had formed an eddy, where the current was strong, and the water deep and dark. We plunged our paddles into the water for a couple backstrokes, but the force was not enough. The river swept us backwards, and we crashed into the foliage overhead.

"Paddle forward now," I said, scrambling for the T grip of my paddle. I tried to dig the blade into the water, but it hit the shoreline to my left. We tugged at the vines and brambles around us, bringing dead leaves and a few spiders drifting into our boat. We slowly inched out from the eddy. In a few seconds, we were back on the main river with twigs and spiderwebs adorning our bodies. Crushed remnants of our crash stirred in murky water sloshing in the bottom of the kayak.

"You OK, guys?" Mom quipped.

Palm Springs Entrance

"I think so," I responded. Suddenly, I felt a sharp sting on my foot.

"ANTS!" We glanced down at the bottom of the boat, where a colony of ants had landed during our crash. We probably dislodged them from their hideout in some hollow bamboo. These were no black ants—they were fire ants. Angry fire ants. Some wobbled on the water's surface as we tried to splash them out, only to regain their footing and skitter back to our feet.

"I see the bridge coming up. We need to stop at the spring!"

We quickly paddled forward and continued to stomp ants left and right. Sure enough, the concrete bridge appeared to our left, marking the entrance of Palm Springs. A couple of girls were sitting on the stairs leading into the spring pool and were surprised to see the two of us in our kayaks, surging through the open gate, arms and legs flailing. Dad and I pulled towards the shallow area of the spring and quickly jumped from the kayak. Mom cruised over the main boil to wait for us.

"Let's just flood the kayak, flip it over, and wash all the ants out," suggested Dad. Easy to say, but not so easy to do. With one person on each end of the craft, we angled it upwards and dumped out the invading insects. To be sure, Dad banged the kayak against the concrete retaining wall to make sure there were no remaining invaders. Finally returned to our pre-crash state, we quietly exited the spring and returned home. The girls had been silent the whole time, but I'm sure we gave them a lot to talk about after we left.

ADVENTURES ON THE LITTLE WEKIVA RIVER

57

LITTLE WEKIVA MEMORIES

Palm Springs is always a welcome retreat, regardless of your reason for being there. Whether its a way station to regroup while on the river, a place to explore, a spot to play, or a visual reminder of adventures enjoyed in decades past, Palm Springs is a great place to visit.

Starbuck Spring

Starbuck Spring always held a certain mystery for me. Every time we kayaked past the run, the crystalline waters seemed to draw me in.

The SJRWMD describes Starbuck as a second-magnitude spring with milky blue water flowing from a single limestone vent. "The circular pool is about 65 to 70 feet in diameter and about 4 to 7 feet deep, with a sandy bottom."[14]

Starbuck Run is clustered with lily-pads, low hanging branches, and the constant flow of clear blue water. Beyond the short outflow is Starbuck Spring, a large, circular pool withheld from the Little Wekiva by a concrete weir. We have never swum in the private spring itself, but I've taken aerial photos with the permission of the current property owner.

Despite the size and quality of the spring, it hasn't shifted hands as many times as nearby Palm and Sanlando. Its recent history began in 1883 when the Altamonte Hotel acquired what was then Shepherd Spring as a picnic and bathing destination for guests. According to Rick Kilby's *Florida's Healing Waters*, "In an 1883 promotional booklet titled 'Orangeland', the author marveled at the crystal waters of Shepherd and nearby Hoosier Springs and asserted that bathing in the spring water, or drinking it, was beneficial to 'patients troubled with rheumatism or blood disease because it was full of sulfur and other minerals'."[5] The hotel continued to use the site through at least 1910.

It's difficult to pinpoint exactly when the Altamonte Hotel stopped taking their guests to Shepherd Spring. What seems clear is that by the time the Yale and Barker families began visiting the site in the 1940s, it had long been left to nature.

Bates family brewing coffee at Shepherd Spring (State Library and Archives of Florida)

The University of South Florida conducted an interview with former owners Don and Jinny Barker in 2001. The narrative explains that Don Barker met a local man during his time with the Civilian Pilot Training Program in 1942, when, shortly after, "this man from Lake Brantley challenged Don's knowledge of Florida and took him to visit Shepherd Spring" In the early days of their visits, the area around the springs was a wild marshland that Jinny Barker described as open marsh. "The water would be anywhere from ankle-deep to knee-deep. It was mucky. I was scared to death of it because of snakes… [The property was also] heavily wooded…The types of trees near Starbuck Spring include bottlebrush, swamp maple, palm, hickory, plum, holly, scrub oak, and long needle pine."[15]

Don and Jinny Barker (Donna Emerson)

Because of the natural beauty, both the Barkers and their surrogate parents, the Yales, fell in love with the area. In 1944, the Yales purchased the land and renamed the spring after their son, Starbuck. Starbuck Yale, a college friend of Don Barker, encouraged Don to move to Florida. After a struggle with leukemia, Starbuck passed away, but the Yale's passion for the springs sparked Don's love for the wild beauty of Florida. The elder Yales owned Starbuck Spring until their deaths, after which Don and Jinny Barker purchased the property in 1964. The Barker family owns Starbuck Spring to this day.

The Barkers had limited knowledge of the history of their property, but Jinny thought that the previous owner was happy to sell the land because it was not good for citrus. There were also stories of an old Masonic Lodge held in a sawmill adjacent to the spring. "On the edge of the Barkers' property there is the foundation of an old building. Jinny speculates that this could have been related to the mill or possibly a citrus grove."[15] Boy Scout groups were also known to have camped out near the hidden spring. Even though the exact history of Starbuck Spring isn't perfectly mapped out, the reports of Masonic activity, Boy Scout visits, and citrus farms paint a colorful story.

Half a mile south, Sanlando Springs Tropical Park was going through changes. According to Robin Sheldon, granddaughter of Moses Overstreet, Mr and Mrs. J. E. Robinson leased the property around Sanlando Springs from the Overstreets in 1950. The park remained under the management of the Robinsons for 20 years until it was purchased by Mr. Earl Downs in 1970. Downs sought to create a sprawling neighborhood that provided homes for Floridians while retaining the natural beauty of spring and forest.

When Downs and his investment team purchased the nearby land, the Barker property, which includes Starbuck Spring remained private. Downs acquired Sanlando Tropical Park, as well as the forested land on the west bank of the Little Wekiva, for his development. 50 years have passed since The Springs was founded. One of the major draws for this neighborhood has been its preservationist mindset and respect for nature. As soon as you drive inside the gates, you feel like the rest of the busy world has fallen away.

Entrance to The Springs neighborhood (circa 2025)

My discoveries about our local history and the geography of the Little Wekiva River made me want to explore more, so when our friend Sue gave us a map displaying a satellite shot of the Wekiva River basin, I became even more invested. Yellow markings signified the location of towns, landings, state parks, and springs. We hung the map in our mud room. Every day after school I would glance at it, laughing at the odd names: Blueberry, Ginger Ale, Moccasin, Tram, Sharkstooth. I also noticed that there were five springs marked quite close to us. These included Sanlando Springs, the large, well-manicured swimming spot by the neighborhood clubhouse, and Palm Springs, the swimming hole at the end of a nearby cul-de-sac. Besides the two we frequented, there were more. Also on the Little Wekiva were Ginger Ale Springs, Pegasus Spring, and Starbuck Spring. Starbuck Spring we knew was owned by the Barkers, but we had no knowledge of the other two sites.

The map showed the Wekiva River Basin from overhead. The densely forested area, most of which is part of Wekiva Springs State Park, is an example of land preserved for its environmental and cultural importance. The stories, secrets, and experiences found in areas like the Wekiva River Basin are important to learn about and understand, especially for locals. In my search for the last two springs, I didn't expect to discover so many interesting things about the area I live in. I learned about history, ecology, community, and more. Beneath the Florida landscape were stories and experiences much more interesting than I could have imagined.

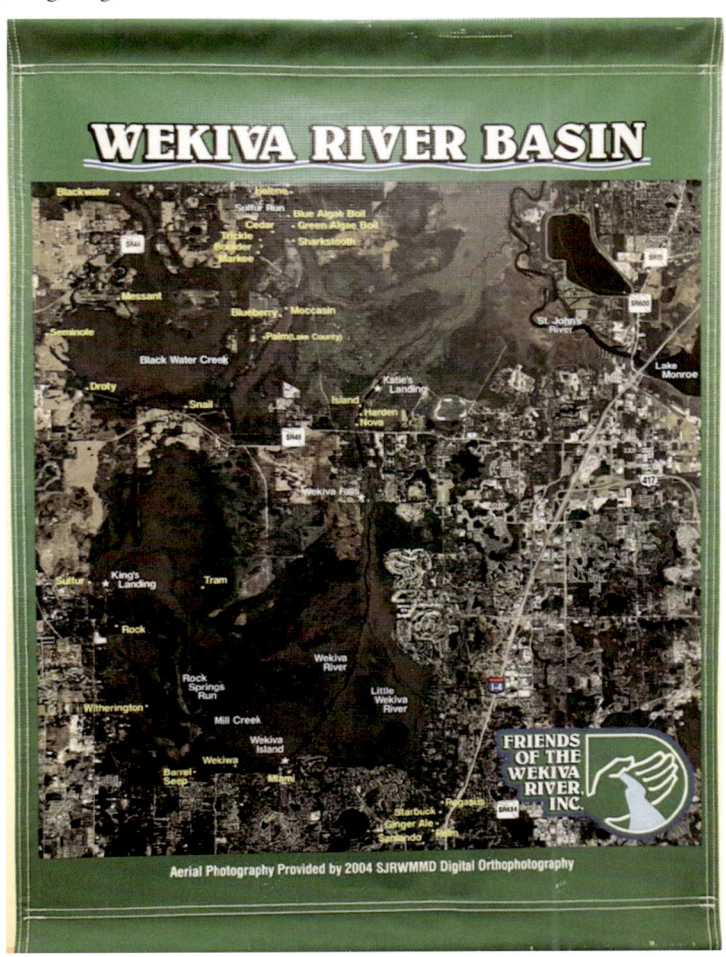

Map of springs Wekiva River Basin

Ginger Ale Springs

The quest to find Ginger Ale Springs began as many trips on the river do, relaxed and laid back as we paddled slowly up stream. As we pushed along against the gentle current, I was thinking about the information I had scoured from the internet. I knew that based on the SJRWMD's entry "Ginger Ale Springs," I should expect a spring pool enclosed by a circular concrete wall. The spring run "flows northwest . . . about 550 feet long and 3 feet wide to the Little Wekiva River."[16] A helpful GPS coordinate was also provided that placed Ginger Ale Springs someplace between Palm Springs and our house, right next to Markham Woods Road.

Our "Friends of the Wekiva River" map also seemed to corroborate this location. As we kayaked further upriver, I kept my eye out for possible tributaries and offshoots that could be Ginger Ale Run. Just as we passed a section clogged with brush and tall grass, a small opening in the riverbank caught my eye.

"Let's check this out," I remarked. Dad and I pointed our kayaks to the shore. Mom decided to stay and wait for us in the creek. We pushed aside a few brambles and began to walk into the forest. The tributary began shallow and solid. A tiny flow of water sloshed its way over the sandy bottom as we followed its path. The feathery vegetation on either side of the tributary soon became shoulder-height as the water level increased. Slowly, the firm, sandy bottom became a little less stable. After sinking my foot into a particularly deep spot of mud, I decided to walk along the side of the tributary instead of in it. As we approached a fork in the path, I heard a splash ahead of me.

"Don't come in!" shouted Dad. Thick mud had grabbed him, pulling him down to his waist. He seemed to be sinking deeper.

"Is everything alright back there?" I heard Mom shouting from the river. She'd noticed the clear run of water flowing into the river turn a dark chocolate brown. Wondering what was going on in the woods, she'd called out to us.

Dad was still flailing in the mud trying to push himself upright as I found a stick to try and stretch out toward him. "I got it," he panted. In a few moments, he lunged from his position and grabbed hold of a branch on the opposite bank. The even distribution of his body weight helped to settle the mud, and he slowly dragged himself to safety. The struggle had caked his entire body with black sludge.

Photo of tributary Ginger Ale

Quicksand, like the Bermuda Triangle and Black Holes, was a danger that seemed real and frightening in my young mind. As I grew older, I realized that such obscure threats were not often encountered. I felt concerned, and a little bit excited, to realize that a "mythic danger" such as quicksand could be found so close to home. We later researched this phenomena and discovered that this specific type of mud was similar in type to pluff mud. Pluff mud is common in estuaries, swamps, and marshlands where decaying organic material mixes with fast moving sediment. The dense, fine material is excellent for the ecosystem and terrible for anyone trying to walk through it! To identify this mud, look out for dull black sediment on the swamp floor. It often has a layer of decaying leaves on top. The swampland between the Little Wekiva and Markham Woods Road provides the perfect environment for pluff mud.

We did not make the mistake of walking through the marshy run ever again, but we did make the mistake of assuming that the tributary was a dead end. We eventually discovered Ginger Ale by a land route. Later, upon further exploration with friends, we realized that the quicksand tributary would have led us straight to Ginger Ale Springs.

The area around Ginger Ale is interesting. The sandy run has a pinkish tinge from minerals in the water. A school of minnows lives within the cement pool as well as a large cat fish hanging out near the main boil. There are several small sand boils bubbling at the bottom of the pool also. Assorted trinkets, charms, grimy religious icons, shampoo bottles, and rags hang from nearby palm trees. From the looks of things, it seems that some visitors treat the spot as a shrine while others treat it as a bathing hole or rest stop. Once at the spring, you can hear Markham Woods Road nearby. We were surprised to discover how easy the spring is to access from the street; a narrow footpath winds down to the spot from behind a concrete cistern. The route from the river is a much more adventurous one.

On another trip up the river with friends, we decided to stop at Ginger Ale. Out of all the springs, this one seems the sketchiest. Its proximity to the road means that anyone can access the area for whatever purpose. Oddly, a flimsy, foldable, metal chair sat by the concrete pool. As we made our way beyond the spring and up toward the roadway, a bedraggled man walked up to us with a beer bottle in hand.

"Watch out for the man in the pickup truck," he warned, "you don't want to be alone when he's nearby." Needless to say, we did not wait for the return of the pickup truck or stay around to chat with the man who gave us the ominous warning.

Despite uncomfortable moments, we appreciated the strange beauty and adventure found around Ginger Ale Springs which we discovered has a far more interesting past.

When Lester Beeman purchased Ms. Saunder-Massey's land in 1916 (excluding what was then called Hoosier Springs), he was focused on Palm Springs. He also discovered a small, unnamed spring deep in the forest. Although the area was not right for a swimming spot, the enterprising Beeman still saw an opportunity for business.

Cat fish

Huston family and friend at Ginger Ale Spring (Huston Family)

Beeman's Ginger Ale (thejaxsonmag.com)

He soon enclosed the boil with a circular concrete tub, which is still standing today, and set up a small bottling plant. According to the Florida History Blog, "The buildings are long gone, but they were probably just uphill from the spring near the roadway and railroad track (now the Seminole-Wekiva Trail)."[7]

Lester's new ginger ale company, Beeman's Mild Dry Ginger Ale, was launched and marketed across the Interstate 4 corridor in Central Florida with the intention to be a nationwide product. Beeman's advertisement claimed that, "In a short time, it is expected it will be in as great demand . . . as are Coca-Cola." Despite the claims, the ale was not a huge success, nor was the "fresh spring water" dredged from the same source. Still, the mineral water and soda "was carried by most local druggists and independent grocers, as well as emerging chains such as United Markets grocery."[7]

In 1935, Beeman finally lost the property around the springs for good. His bottling company went defunct, and the only remnant of that time is the concrete retaining wall surrounding Ginger Ale Springs.

Pegasus Spring

The search for Pegasus Spring was significantly more difficult than we had expected. Palm Springs, Sanlando Springs, Starbuck Spring, and even Ginger Ale Springs were all at least partially developed and set apart. They each played roles in the local community at some point and were marked and established accordingly. On the other end of the spectrum was Pegasus Spring. Based on my research, I could find almost no historical record of ownership for this spring. It was only recorded in the SJRWMD's "Pegasus Spring" entry as "a third magnitude spring," with the spring head described as, "a small pool with the vent discharging at an angle."[17] The only additional information I discovered was that a sand boil is also present approximately 200 feet down the spring run, and semitropical forests surround the spring. These descriptors could have been attributed to most springs in the area.

The picture on the website depicted a spring pool so densely surrounded by foliage that I could not draw any information from it. The only helpful information I noticed from the picture was a location marking. Starbuck Spring was described as, "less than 0.1 mile toward the northwest. Ginger Ale Springs and Palm Springs (were) located 0.3 and 0.4 mile, respectively, toward the south-southwest from Pegasus Spring." My problems began there. I knew of Pegasus Spring only because of the "Friends of the Wekiva River" map hanging in our mudroom. According to that map, Pegasus Spring was the northernmost spring on the Little Wekiva River, well past Starbuck. This contradicted the placement of Pegasus being between Starbuck and Ginger Ale as described online. We decided to stick with the map.

Pegasus Spring (SJRWMD)

Little Wekiva Memories

Drone picture of downriver

The journey began on a Sunday afternoon with a few of my friends. For the first time, we decided to travel downriver from my house instead of upriver. Although it was theoretically easier to go downriver due to the current, a low-lying bridge discouraged us from trying. Fortunately, the water level was low enough that we could crouch down in our kayaks and slide under the crumbling beams of the bridge. As we drifted further downstream, we watched the scenery change. Dense semi-tropical forestland gave way to a more marshy, open "savannah." Further downriver, deciduous trees like oak and swamp maple, became more prominent. We also discovered several spots where swiftly moving water had carved deep pools in the riverbed. Wooden planks were nailed into overhanging trees so that people could jump into the deep spots. Farther along, the river opened up, allowing a wider view of our surroundings. I felt a sense of adventure meeting each twist and turn not knowing what to expect around the bend. Despite the new experience, we were not able to find any offshoots or tributaries that might have been Pegasus Run. Not long after passing under the Springs Estate road, swamp grass choked out the river, and we were forced to return home. Back to the drawing board.

ADVENTURES ON THE LITTLE WEKIVA RIVER

I returned to my research and decided to map out what I'd discovered so far, exactly to scale. I placed Starbuck Springs and Ginger Ale Springs 0.4 miles apart, as described online. I also marked a point representing Pegasus Spring 0.1 miles south of Starbuck. This visual aid helped me realize that Pegasus Spring was much closer than I first imagined. I had been passing its outflow for years without realizing it. I also found an *Orlando Sentinel* article from 2005, detailing the journey of Lou Ley, the geographic information systems coordinator for the Florida Department of Environmental Protection. According to the article, "Ley [was] working on the Florida Springs Initiative, a long-term study designed to further the understanding of these windows into the aquifer."[18] His job included, "finding and mapping 'rediscovered' springs — from small boils that bubble up almost imperceptibly from river bottoms to large springs once visited by thousands of tourists but now hidden from the public within gated communities."[18] Pegasus, revisited by UCF professors in the 1990s, was on his list of springs to find.

I was excited to hear about another adventurer's search for Pegasus. What didn't excite me was the path towards the spring described as "snake-and-alligator-infested that border the Little Wekiva." Ley and his team entered the swamp from Markham Woods Road and "donned their waders" to "follow the flow of the shallow channels back to their source." What I gleaned from the Sentinel article was that anyone looking for a well-defined "run" to trace back to its source would be disappointed. Pegasus Spring Run, "rather than following a defined channel . . . spreads out and flows sheetlike toward the river."[18]

Armed with expectations and new information, I reconvened with some friends and headed upstream to find Pegasus Spring. We were within earshot of my home, just one bend of the river past Starbuck Run, when we spotted a tiny stream bed. Although I'd seen the spot before, I never interpreted it as a spring run, since the outflow was only a trickle. We pulled our kayaks onto the sandy bank and slowly forged a path along the shallow run.

ADVENTURES ON THE LITTLE WEKIVA RIVER

On the hunt for Pegasus Spring

LITTLE WEKIVA MEMORIES

"This seems pretty straightforward to me," I thought. *"If this is Pegasus Run, it certainly doesn't seem sheetlike."* The woods seemed to fill with more clear, spring-fed water as we advanced further. In a few minutes, we emerged into a more open area with fern-covered ground and a higher canopy.

"It opens up ahead," mentioned my friend Micah.

Sure enough, the narrow stream quickly lost itself in a sheetlike, swampy run. We spent a few more minutes picking our way from dry spot to dry spot, following the flow of the water, and exploring the area, but we eventually decided to turn back, since we were not well equipped to get in the "snake-and-alligator-infested swamplands" quite yet. Still, we discovered Pegasus Spring Run, and were excited about our adventure near one of Florida's rare gems!

Due to the hidden nature of Pegasus Spring, and the limited information about it online, it was difficult to trace the spot's history. Perhaps it truly was undeveloped and unknown for most of recent history. Chances are that either Ingram Fletcher, Elizabeth Saunders-Massey, or Frank Haithcox had Pegasus Spring on their property at one point, but they never utilized it, shared its location, or even knew it was there.

Perhaps it is best left in obscurity as "untouched" springs are incredibly rare. Most of Florida's springs are contained by concrete walls, surrounded by development, and frequented by visitors. Pegasus Spring is an example of the hidden beauty so often lost when humans try to direct nature towards their own motives and intentions. Springs are for healing, appreciation, respect, and preservation. To diminish their role is to endanger their existence. As Rick Kilby explains in his book, *Florida's Healing Waters*, "early in the twenty-first century it became apparent that these 'bowls of liquid light' faced a dark future due to over-tapping of the aquifer and increasing pollution." Furthermore, "Nitrogen from fertilizer seeps into the aquifer from both agricultural and residential sources and often pollutes spring water."[5] These changes can lead to unhealthy, "gunky" water. Algae and other forms of pollution create unsightly growth in the once crystal, clear water.

Our interference with nature has led to these dangerous changes in the water system, so it's our

job as Floridians to repair our natural resources and take care of our state's beautiful and unique water source. By caring for and learning about our springs, we preserve their allure, mystery, and beauty for generations to come. Learning about our local history helps us understand who we are as Floridians, where we've come from, and just what we have to cherish. Lessons can be learned from the past that help ensure our safety and the safety of our natural resources, in the future.

Several organizations are committed to preserving these natural resources. The St. Johns River Water Management District (SJRWMD) is a government organization that oversees the St. Johns Watershed. According to its website's main page, "In its daily operations, the district tries to strike a balance in water needs by educating the public about water conservation, setting rules for water use, conducting research, collecting data, restoring and protecting water above and below the ground, and preserving natural areas."[19] If you are interested in finding easy ways to help keep springs safe and clean, there are many strategies explained on the website. Running your sprinklers less frequently or being intentional about your landscaping choices help to decrease your water usage and keeps our rivers healthy.

Another organization, the Friends of the Wekiva River, is focused specifically on conservation within the Wekiva River Basin. The map provided by this organization is what inspired me to explore my area more thoroughly. Their efforts involve preventing problems like "the fragmentation and loss of habitat, declines in spring flow, degradation in water quality, and wildlife mortality on the roads." Organization members "work on issues that affect the Wekiva, ranging from pollution to smart growth to the welfare of wildlife, including bears."[20] As you can see, conservation goes beyond monitoring chemical pollution or restricting water waste. Being more aware of how each plant and animal influences the balance of an ecosystem can help efforts as well.

Although there are several groups dedicated to protecting our rivers and springs, and many individuals working to better inform Floridians, making real change is difficult unless people like you and me are willing to be intentional about our impact on the environment. As you enjoy the natural beauty around you, remember that a pristine landscape requires care to maintain.

ADVENTURES ON THE LITTLE WEKIVA RIVER

*Come along with me as I share memories of adventures on the Little Wekiva River.
I know you will grow to appreciate the springs, the river, and the history of Central Florida more fully.*

Life along the Little Wekiva

LEIF AND I JOIN COUNTLESS OTHERS WHO HAVE FOUND THE LITTLE WEKIVA RIVER AND ITS TRIBUTARIES TO BE BEAUTIFULLY MYSTERIOUS.
—NICHOLE

Looking back several years ago, with a move to Florida facing us, we were on the hunt for a place to call home. When I turned into The Springs near Interstate 4 and State Road 434, I was intrigued. The neighborhood felt a little wild to me. Wild is the word that comes to mind because many of the communities we had been looking at were more manicured and open. As I drove around Springs Boulevard, large oaks arched over the road. Native plants ruled. A gently curving road carried me for a full mile to the far edge of the neighborhood. We pulled into the driveway of a beautiful home surrounded by grand trees and lush landscape, but what took our breath away was the backyard with its gradual slope ending at the banks of a little creek. It was a rainy day in February, and, as Floridians know, after a rain, the plants seem to sprout several inches of electric green foliage overnight. I'd come from the cold and snow of Washington D.C., but weather in Florida was balmy. Peacocks were cawing and preening in the yard.

This all was a radical change. My senses were scrambling to make the adjustments. Leif, who was two at the time, spotted a frog hopping in the grass. He was off, chasing after the little guy, matching each jump with a hop of his own. The unfamiliar landscape seemed to be casting a siren's call. Jeff and I were captivated. This felt like the right place to raise our family.

We have come to treasure our spot on the Little Wekiva more than we thought possible. Through the years, Leif and I have also developed an interest in the history along this stretch of the river. The more time we spend paddling and exploring, the more we discover. We have been enriched by conversations with others who also revel in the landscape. The stories they shared were at times nostalgic, always surprising, and overflowing with love for life on the river and around the springs. These conversations highlight the lives of those who have made an impact on the region, helping us trace the history of development along the Little Wekiva River Basin.

Moses Overstreet born Kirkland, GA 1869—1955 Orlando, FL (State Library and Archives of Florida)

Historical Marker Sylvan Lake Park

Robin Sheldon is a descendant of the Overstreet family that figures prominently in the history of Central Florida. The Overstreet Land Company owned much of the property along the Little Wekiva River. This included the land that surrounded Sanlando and Palm Springs.

Moses Overstreet moved from Georgia to Plymouth, Florida in 1898 when the turpentine company he worked for expanded its operations into Florida. It was not long before the ambitious Moses became the sole owner of the company, changing its name to the Overstreet Turpentine Company. At the time, the turpentine industry was thriving in Seminole County. Turpentine was used extensively for solvents, paints, and even for medicinal purposes. Gum was collected in cups placed below a slash in a pine tree. The tall, native pines in Florida were an excellent source of gum that, when heated, could easily be separated into turpentine, tar, and rosin. A historical marker in Sanford's Sylvan Lake Park pays tribute to the turpentine industry in Central Florida. The Overstreet Turpentine Company is highlighted as a leading company in the early 20th century.

Plymouth was an unincorporated area in Orange County, northwest of downtown Apopka. It was here that Moses met his future wife, Ethelyn. In 1903, they moved to Orlando. Their granddaughter, Robin, shared some family stories with me. "My grandfather started buying lots of land along Markham Woods Road and all over Sanford and in downtown Orlando." The entrepreneurial young man was savvy, funding his property investments with money made from other business ventures. Besides turpentine, Moses invested in Florida's flourishing citrus business. In 1908, he started the Overstreet Crate Company where he ran a sawmill that manufactured shipping crates used by many of Central Florida's citrus growers. The family also owned acres of orange and grapefruit trees. Robin remembers her father telling stories of working in the family's groves as a young man.

Moses worked to expand his real-estate business and changed his company's name to the Overstreet Investment Company in 1923. The company eventually owned over 25,000 acres throughout Florida. A unique purchase included hundreds of acres along the Little Wekiva River, including springs that flowed into the river. In 1925, Frank Haithcox negotiated with Overstreet for a land lease on property surrounding what was then called Hoosier Springs. The Florida Midland Railroad followed the old wagon trail that ran from Longwood to Apopka, and the station along the route was within easy walking distance to the spring. Haithcox began developing the area around the spring by enclosing one side with a cement walkway. An online article on *Historic Longwood* describes Haithcox's improvements. By damming the spring, he was able to block the river from flowing into the springs, thereby containing the flow which created a larger spring fed pool. With the addition of a pumping station, he was able to fill his new cement swimming pool with water from Sanlando Springs. He then changed the name of the spring and called his new park Sanlando Springs. The park soon became a favorite destination for local families.[21]

Overstreet shipping crate. (Overstreet Family)

Overstreet Development Advertisements (Overstreet Family)

LITTLE WEKIVA MEMORIES

The Senator. (State Library and Archives of Florida)

In the meantime, Moses was developing other interests. He became president of the Peoples National Bank while still managing the Overstreet Investment Co. real estate ventures. He also served the city and state in many offices, including Orange County Commissioner, and two terms as a Florida State Senator during the 1920s. Senator Overstreet donated several acres of land to Seminole County for use as a park. The land was filled with pine and cypress trees. One tree in particular, an ancient bald cypress, would be the centerpiece of the park. "Big Tree" was estimated to be over 3,500 years old. Upon the park's dedication in 1929, presided over by President Calvin Coolidge, the tree was renamed in honor of Senator Moses Overstreet. Tragically, "The Senator" was lost in a devastating fire in 2012.[22]

Moses and Ethelyn had four children. Robert "Bob", Hazel, Elizabeth, and Mildred. As their family was growing and Moses was building a personal legacy in Central Florida, the legacy surrounding the springs on the Little Wekiva continued to grow. It was the early 1930s. Frank Haithcox, like many people in America, was struggling financially due to the Great Depression and was forced to relinquish his Sanlando Springs land lease. The property reverted back to the Overstreet Land Company.

Bob Overstreet was developing a special interest in Sanlando Springs and had all sorts of ideas for what could be done to build on Haithcox's improvements. He imagined extensive gardens, walking trails, improved facilities, and exciting activities that would continue to attract people from Florida and beyond. Robin shared a letter her father wrote in 1948 to his sister, Mildred, in it Bob recalled how he became involved in the Sanlando Springs project. "I persuaded Papa to sell...for he would not consent to spending

Robert Overstreet. 1902–1992 (Overstreet Family)

any money [on the springs]". Father and son agreed to a purchase price of $5000. Bob invested personal money to continue beautifying the property by creating a large sandy beach, and updating the facilities. Above the spring he laid a terrazzo dance floor. Speakers were hung in one of the large oak trees whose branches stretched over the patio.

On February 27th, 1937, the *Orlando Morning Sentinel* heralded the "Formal Opening of Sanlando Springs." The event was packed with swimming and diving exhibitions and a fashion show would feature "spectacular gowns and beach styles." Bandleader Eddie Stephenson and his orchestra, the Florida Rhythm King Boys, played on the lawn while guests took to the dance floor. News clippings from the Overstreet family chronicle the grand opening. The *Sentinel* featured a full-page advertisement with one of the pictures highlighting three models who starred in the "Fashion Revue." A very beautiful Sara Harris stands confidently, looking directly at the camera, her elegant bathing-suit cover billowing around her long legs. Her megawatt smile and those legs caught the attention of Bob Overstreet.

Special events continued to pack the calendar in the months that followed. One memorable guest was Katherine Rawls. In the 1930s, Katie Rawls was considered "the greatest woman swimmer." The *Seminole Spotlight* explains in a February 2008 article that she "not only swam but was a diver as well… At age fourteen, she won a silver medal in springboard diving at the 1932 Olympics held in Los Angeles… She won another Silver Medal in springboard diving at the Berlin Olympics in 1936." This beloved Florida girl wowed crowds at Sanlando Springs in May of 1937.[23]

Katherine Rawls Advertisement May 1937 (Overstreet Family)

Diver at the Springs (Overstreet Family)

Sanlando Springs Fashion Models 1937 Sara Harris Center right (Overstreet Family)

Lovely ladies posing at the spring, late 1930s early 1940s (Overstreet Family)

Throughout the late 1930s, Sara Harris, that lovely swimsuit model, worked with Bob in the Orange County Criminal Court where he was the clerk. He hired her as his secretary, and a romance blossomed into a marriage in 1943.

During World War II, while Robert was serving in the Navy, his dreams for Sanlando Park were kept alive with help from his mother Ethelyn. The park hosted GIs from McCoy Air Force Base in Orlando, creating many happy memories for soldiers stationed locally or just passing through.

After the war, Bob committed more time and money to renovations, further revitalizing Sanlando Springs Tropical Park. *The Sunday Sentinel-Star* reported in an article shortly after WWII that "Robert T. Overstreet nourished his dream…of making Sanlando Springs a resort on a par with Silver Springs, Cypress Gardens and other premier attractions of the state." He invested in creating beautifully landscaped garden areas with azaleas and shallow pools filled with water lilies. A clubhouse and dining room offering lunch and evening dinners was added. M. J. Daetwyler, a family friend and renowned local landscape designer, was hired to continue beautification of the gardens surrounding the spring and along the river. More azaleas and camellias were added, making it "the largest gardens of its kind in Florida."[24]

LIFE ALONG THE LITTLE WEKIVA

Canoeing on the Little Wekiva 1930s early 1940s (Overstreet Family)

Whimsically creative advertising shared news about all that Sanlando Springs had to offer. A brochure with colorful cartoon drawings enticed guests to set out on adventurous "Jungle Cruises" to explore gardens full of beautiful flowers, relax and sunbathe on white, sandy beaches, and explore tropical gardens along the shore of the river. The swimming pool and its bath house were popular, but the highlight, of course, was cooling off in the blue waters of the spring.

Advertisement Sanlando Springs (Overstreet Family)

Palm Springs vintage 1930s/40s (Overstreet Family)

Overgrown surroundings at Palm Springs, 1930s/40s (Overstreet Family)

In July of 1944, the Overstreets acquired Palm Springs and merged it with their Sanlando Springs Park. Cottages near Palm Springs were rented to guests who spent several weeks at a time vacationing near the iconic sulfur spring. The idea was to bring Palm Springs back to some of its former glory, however it never again eclipsed, or even matched, the level of development that Sanlando Springs now offered. Lily pads and catfish were taking over, and Sanlando Springs was the place to be!

A conversation with Robin, her cousin Marcia Harris Voorhees, and Marcia's daughter Sara, offered a fun glimpse of life around the springs in the late 1940s. Marcia worked at the park as a young girl helping with odd jobs. Ethelyn, who still enjoyed keeping an eye on business at the park, would pick up Marcia in her car. Marcia and the hot dog warmer shared a backseat on the drive to the springs. After arriving, Ethelyn would set the young girl up at an outdoor stand selling hot dogs for 15 cents apiece. Marcia remembered a certain group of visitors at Sanlando Springs who had come from out of town that had heard about the famous playground and were intrigued. They explored the grounds, surprised and delighted by the unique setting, the magical garden paradise, the pristine springs, and all the adventurous things to do in the water. There was that magnificent slide! The big diving board! Clear, turquoise water enticed them, but, unfortunately they did not have bathing suits with them. Ethelyn remembered that in years past, bathing suits were available to rent at Palm Springs. Thinking there might be some suits left in the cottages by the old

Tall slide at Sanlando Spring, 1940s (Overstreet Family)

resort, she took the guests along for the short walk from Sanlando to Palm Springs. Pushing open the door to one of the cabins, the musty heat of a long-enclosed space greeted them. After rummaging through a few boxes, they hit the jackpot: rubber bathing suits! Imagining the scene, we had to laugh. The rubber suits must have been sticky after years folded in cardboard boxes, stored in the heat and humidity of an abandoned cabin—long before air conditioning. The ladies probably had a time of it, peeling the suits apart and shimmying into them. Regardless, it got them into the beautiful spring—and on that huge slide! The anticipation was high as they climbed the ladder that seemed to go on forever. They skidded and lurched down the slide in those rubber suits. But, before hitting the water, the rubber caught on something, ripping a hole in the suit! I can only imagine the return trip to the bathhouse as the women tried to hold that rubber suit together.

*R.T. and Sara Overstreet, 1940s
(Overstreet Family)*

Bob and his wife Sara had two girls, Anne and Robin. Marcia remembers Bob, Sara, and Anne, an infant at the time, living in one of the cabins in the woods near Sanlando Springs. This was before Robin was born, so she has no memory of this time. According to a family letter Bob wrote in 1948, he intended to continue to run Sanlando Springs after the war, but when an opportunity arose for him to lease the property, he was glad to make the deal. Sara found the commute from Sanlando Springs into the city to doctor's offices and shops challenging, and Bob's growing involvement with the Overstreet Land Company kept him busy elsewhere. The family moved to Orlando.

J.E. Robinson negotiated a lease with the Overstreet Land Co. to run Sanlando Springs Tropical Park. Robinson continued to run the operation for the next twenty years just as the Overstreet and Haithcox families had done before him.[25]

Robin remembers how much her mother loved the river and the springs. After moving back to Orlando, "my Dad bought land on Lake Butler that we used as a retreat. My mother thought the lake water was too warm during Florida's hot summers." The cool, refreshing water of the spring-fed Little Wekiva River was luring them back to the Sanlando Springs area. Bob bought several acres from the family land company, creating a retreat on the banks of the Little Wekiva.

*Overstreet dinner at the "camp"
(Overstreet Family)*

*Mom "Sara" and Anne on bridge 1963
(Overstreet Family)*

Family and friends enjoyed time together at their "camp." Huge dinners were savored on the patio of their little house in the woods. While eating, they reveled in expansive views of the grassy slope and river beyond. Another generation was making memories by the river.

Robin's childhood memories come easily to her. "We would go out to the camp on weekends." She remembers idyllic days playing among tall pines and old oaks with her sister. They took meandering walks with their mother, collecting violet bouquets along the way. Sara helped train their eyes to notice the beauty in nature. They found treasures in tree bark, plants, and fossils. "Even as children, we knew how special our time by the river was."

Robin and her cousin riding along the Little Wekiva River (Overstreet Family)

Launching from their backyard, they floated downriver, fishing as they drifted past tall grasses. When not playing in the spring-fed river, the girls would spend their days riding horses, Anne on Sparky and Robin on Rebel—"the crazy one." The girls rode for miles. "We'd cross through the woods, along the creek, all the way to Lake Brantley, and along the Little Wekiva River."

"We had lots of animals!" Robin laughed as she talked of the flock of chickens that wandered their property. "We had a rooster named Bill who was mean as the dickens! We lived in fear of his vicious attacks. He mysteriously disappeared after a few years." One of their long-necked geese chose to lay her eggs by the front door, so people coming to the house had to stop and pay their respects as they stepped over the goose. One of those eggs was taken to the high school and popped into the incubator. Before long, a little gosling hatched, becoming Beverly Barker's favorite pet. The children all loved "Gus the Goose." The Barker family lived near the Overstreets in Orlando. The Barker's retreat on the Little Wekiva River was also near the Overstreet's camp. Robin remembers Beverly driving a golf cart over to their home in town for a visit. Gus the Goose would follow Beverly, flying along behind the cart.

Animals adopted in town would sometimes make the trip with the family to the camp on the weekends. The girls were given a baby raccoon that they named Mary Alice. "She would come round the house for handouts." Mary Alice trailed behind the girls on all their town adventures, learning to ride on the back of Robin's bike. While at the camp Mary Alice waddled after the girls as they ran down to the creek to hunt for shark teeth. Robin and her sister ran their hands through the sand in the creek bed, letting the sand sift through their fingers in hopes of finding a treasure. The raccoon would settle in beside them, digging her little paws through the sand, looking for all the world like she was a serious treasure hunter.

A family of brilliantly colored peacocks were housed in a large aviary at the camp. Their exotic plumage and throaty caw made quite a statement. Bob surprised Sara on her birthday with a dramatic gift of a pair of albino peacocks. The uniquely beautiful white birds made a striking contrast strutting along beside the other birds with their turquoise and green plumage. Eventually, the peacocks escaped their enclosure and had free rein of the property.

Sandlando Tropical Park 1940s (State Library and Archives of Florida)

Besides their animal friends, Robin remembers making friends with other children who lived near the Little Wekiva. Nestled in the dense Florida jungle, on a little rise of land across State Road 434 from what is now the entrance to The Springs community, Robin remembers a primitive house with roots and vines tugging at its foundations. It was bursting at the seams with the large Eustead family who was living off the land just as Florida's early settlers had done in years gone by. She remembers Nellie, Carmelita, and Wilber running through the woods in their bare feet. Their wood framed home had dirt floors and lacked running water. Robin surmises that the family carried water to the house from the river and spring.

Robin, her sister, and their cousins would often play with the Eustead children, traipsing down a winding dirt road to Sanlando Springs Tropical Park. The long slide that sent them on a rocket ride into cool water provided endless hours of fun. Following the smell of sulphur through the jumble of trees and underbrush, they would arrive at the decaying remains of the Palm Springs bathhouse—the perfect backdrop for games fueled by childhood imaginations.

Robin reflected on the marked changes in the landscape over the years. "A two rut road led past the Barkers who lived near us on the river. The road went on down to our camp." On either side of the road, banks that fell into clay pits, providing a messy playground for the kids. "We'd slip and slide our way down the banks, then claw our way back up and do it again." When they finally tired, the cool river cleaned them off. In some ways, the landscape today is unrecognizable when compared to stories from the not too distant past.

Palm springs / cabin 1930s (Overstreet Family)

Over the years, the Overstreet Land Co. sold much of its property which changed the landscape around the Little Wekiva River and the five springs that flow into it. A couple of parcels close to the river were sold to families who used the property as the Overstreet family did—for private retreats. Larger parcels were sold to development companies. On March 15, 1970, Sanlando Springs Tropical Park opened for its final season. The *Sentinel* reported that Earl Downs, head of Downs Properties, purchased the springs and over 320 surrounding acres with plans to develop a mixed-use community.[24] Memory-making at this unique and beloved local playground had come to an end. The favorite family destination would now become the center of Downs's visionary lifestyle community.

The Florida jungle was slowly being subdued. Developments like Sable Point and the Sweetwater communities on Wekiva Springs Road were emerging on land formerly owned by the Overstreet Investment and Land Companies. Overstreet property was developed into Springs Landing in the 1980s. Alaqua Lakes, Wingfield Reserve, and other developments followed along Markham Woods Road.

Businesses, such as Petty's Meat Market, popped up on former Overstreet land. Florida author, Jason Byrne, reflects on changes to the Central Florida landscape in his *Florida History* blog, which highlighted the Pettigrew-Hidalgo family legacy in the area.[26] Petty's opened their Longwood location in November of 1977 near the entrance to, what was then, the new Springs Community. At the time, Earl Downs was concerned about shopping and other conveniences for new residents since there was nothing but trees and scrub brush in the area. Petty's and other grocers, gas stations, and services were moving in around the new developments, all of which changed the landscape along the Little Wekiva River—ushering in a new era.

LITTLE WEKIVA MEMORIES

While much has changed along the Little Wekiva River, it is reassuring to recognize traces of familiarity from the past that remain. The Overstreet family kept a parcel of Moses's original property on the river. The little house that Bob and Sara built still stands by the spring-fed river. Robin continues to make trips out to their camp. Each visit brings a flood of happy memories. Rudy and Bebop, the roosters, welcome the day with their crowing. Descendants of Sara's peacocks can be heard around the neighborhood including a pair of albinos that follow along with the flock, perching on roof peaks and screaming from the tall pines. If the pines could, they would tell tales of resin being tapped from their trunks. These familiar scenes are just a few reminders of the rich history surrounding the Little Wekiva River and the springs flowing into it.

Words put into verse by Sara Overstreet capture feelings of gratitude for this special spot by the river.

A Gracious Prayer
Thank you, God, for sun and showers
Thank you for each stately tree
Thank you for each lovely flower
For thru all these You speak to me.

Along the river (Overstreet Family)

Don and Virginia Barker were longtime landowners of several acres on the Little Wekiva River that included beautiful Starbuck Spring. Together, they created a family sanctuary amid the lush Florida landscape. In the 1940s and 50s, the young couple and their growing family would make the trek out to their camp from Orlando, navigating through woods and dirt roads. Interstate 4 would not be completed through Orlando until the early 1960s, so driving through Maitland and Altamonte Springs on unpaved roads lined with pine and palmetto forests, orange groves, and cow pastures could be a challenge. Their trek took them by the old Altamonte Hotel near Maitland Blvd and Lake Drive. What are now Altamonte Mall and Cranes Roost were then open fields filled with grazing cattle. Finally, an easier route was cut through the wilds: Douglas Avenue, a narrow, orange clay road. This was a welcome alternative unless it rained—then it was impassable.

Don Barker attended the University of Virginia where he made friends with Nathanial Starbuck Yale. "Starbuck" had leukemia, and his parents, originally from upstate New York, were relocating to Florida in hopes that the climate in Florida would be healing. His father, Birch Yale, suffered from the effects of childhood polio and thought he could benefit as well. When Starbuck asked Don to drive him to Florida, their lives were forever changed. The United States joined the war in Europe about this time, and while in Florida, Don joined the Civilian Pilot Training Program based out of McCoy Air Force Base in Orlando. Don fell in love with Florida's wild beauty and warm climate. He never returned to UVA to finish his last year of law school, instead he made Florida his home, becoming an honorary member of the Starbuck family.[15]

When Don spotted Shepherd Spring from the air while out flying, and later explored it by land, he fell in love with the secluded spot. Researching for ownership, he discovered that, because of the war, the property was for sale. The owner had planned to retire in Florida, leaving his business in his son's hands. With his son being drafted, the owner unexpectedly needed to return north. Don excitedly shared his discovery with his good friends the Yales. Birch Yale told Don he would purchase the property with the idea that Don would buy it from the family estate when Birch passed away. By the time Don purchased the property, Shepherd Spring had been renamed Starbuck Spring in honor of Nathanial Starbuck Yale, who had succumbed to his illness.

Little Wekiva Memories

To understand what it was like living along the Little Wekiva River in the 1950s and 60s, you need to imagine a different world where kids were free to explore the river and woods on their own. Huge alligators were found sunning along the banks. Beautiful foxes could be spotted slipping through the woods. Panthers slinked in the shadows. Large snakes hid in thickets. Today's rare bobcat sightings are exciting reminders of long ago days.

In the mid 1950s, the Barker / Yale families watched with alarm as Starbucks Springs went from being swimmable to wadeable. The family speculated that a sinkhole affected the flow. To recreate a swimming hole experience, they dredged a space within the spring area and installed cement bags around the perimeter. At the north and south end of the dam they installed wooden plugs which, at night they would pull the plugs to release the water and clean the swimming hole. Today, the St. Johns Water Management team comes every other month to measure the spring's flow and quality. The water has a slight sulphur element, but not as dramatically as Palm Springs further up the river.

Starbuck Run, 1980s (Sue Tyndall)

A canoe trip downriver from Starbuck Run highlights the ever-changing waterway. Hurricanes and continued development have deeply impacted the Little Wekiva River's delicate, spring-fed ecosystem. For example, water released from Cranes Roost after storms often floods the area.[27]

Invasive vines along the river

In 2004, Hurricane Charley and the three storms that followed it in quick succession changed the landscape drastically. Water flooded the spring runs and ran through the woods for months afterwards. Fallen trees clogged the river, diverting the direction of the Little Wekiva. Downriver, a grass culvert (that was on the property that our family now owns) provided a path across Starbuck Spring Run. This grass bridge washed out and the main river merged with Starbuck Spring Run, drastically shortening the run. For a short distance, the Little Wekiva riverbed is now a swampy thicket, until it rejoins its original path downriver.

In 2017, Hurricane Irma blew across Florida, further impacting the river. Natural disasters and man made ones continue to change the riverscape. Islands separating spring runs from the riverbed are shrinking. When trees topple, they create dams where eddies form deep channels in the riverbed. The flora and fauna are changing as well. Pine, scrub oaks, and palmettos are all being choked by invasive vines.

LIFE ALONG THE LITTLE WEKIVA

One of the biggest changes along this stretch of the river was the development of The Springs community in the 1970s. Four families, including the Barkers, kept their properties by the river instead of selling to Earl Downs and his development group. Starbuck Spring remains protected and private. The Barker family continues to revel in the beauty of their secluded property. Alligators, snapper, gar, and catfish swim in the water. Hawks swoop down to grab their prey. Bears amble across the grass. There's a sense of wonder by the river. A new generation is committed to preserving their spring and their legacy—recognizing that they have a little piece of paradise among the old pines and palmettos. A calmness fills the air when you're resting by Starbuck Spring.

Changes in the Little Wekiva river (Susan Tyndall)

Entrance sign to Sanlando Springs Tropical Park on right (Florida Library and Archives)

Sandra Smith Regal's family was originally from Jacksonville, Florida. They moved to Forest City in 1956. Sandy remembers visiting Sanlando Springs Tropical Park as a child while it was run by J.E. Robinson.

Our family got an annual pass. There were three of us children. Going to the spring was a special treat. Our mother would give each of us a cardboard box and send us into the yard to pick weeds. Our reward for all our hard work was an afternoon at Sanlando Springs. We'd head out into the flower beds with our boxes, filling them quickly and scramble back to our mom, showing her that we were ready to head to the park. She was a smart lady. She'd smash the weeds down and send us back to the garden. When she was satisfied with our work, and the three of us children were hot and dirty, we'd pile into the car.

At this time, State Road 434 was a wooded, two-lane road; Interstate 4 did not exist. Sandy remembers driving through forests and ranch land to get to the park. State Road 436, near today's Congo River Mini Golf, down toward the Olive Garden Restaurant, and up Frances Drive, was open pasture with cattle grazing.

After what seemed like forever, the family car approached the entrance of Sanlando Springs Tropical Park. Everyone's sense of anticipation rose as they drove toward the spring through heavily forested land. Sandy remembers they all loved the huge slide that dumped them into the cool spring, where they spent happy afternoons playing in the water. It was an internal battle as they worked up their nerve to make the steep climb up the stairs of the slide, once again. Seated at the top of the slide, they had the best view in the park. Then, leaning forward slightly, gravity would take over. "It was a thrill ride!" as they swooshed down the slide, landing in the water with a big splash.

Their afternoon adventures included "walks through the camellia and azalea gardens. Bushes were thick with blooms and reached high above our heads. There were native huts along the river." Sandy remembered hearing stories about Tarzan movies being filmed along the Wekiva River near the springs, so their imaginations would run wild with magical tales of adventure as they explored the trails along the river. Most likely, the movie they heard about was *Johnny Tiger*, the 1966 Universal Studios film which was shot in Central Florida. Several scenes were set around Sanlando Springs. Girls would swoon over glimpses of Robert Taylor and Chad Everett filming at the spring. The movie has become a camp classic. Indoor scenes were filmed at Shamrock Studios, formerly on Nicolet Avenue in Winter Park.[28]

"There was an old sulphur spring (Palm Springs) that was scary looking. None of us wanted to swim in that!" Sandy laughed, and a soft smile spread across her face.

Sandy's Grandson, Micah, swimming in Palm Spring, 2023

Slide at Sanlando Springs 1940s
(State Library and Archives of Florida)

"In the evenings there was dancing on a patio near the snack bar. We were all tired after a long day in the sun, but we loved sitting in the grass by the dance floor, watching the couples sway to the music."

Starlight, moonlight, and music cast a romantic spell that seems to have held on in the hearts and minds of those who grew up spending time at the springs. Similar stories emerge when talking to people about their memories of Sanlando Springs Tropical Park. "It was the place to go!" is a common refrain. Adults vividly remember their childhood escapades on the Little Wekiva. While canoeing on the river, it was fun to imagine that you were an explorer lost in the wild. Navigating around a bend, past dense foliage, you would soon find yourself back in the thick of the action on the sandy shore of Sanlando Springs.

Dancing couple 1940s
(State Library and Archives of Florida)

Snack shop, 1940s (State Library and Archives of Florida)

Sandy remembers, "In those days, the park was always crowded. Everybody from the surrounding area came to cool off or take a walk through the gardens." The snack shop was a special treat. People enjoyed ice cream, hot dogs, and hamburgers while sitting under the big oak trees shading the lawn.

By the 1970s, Sandy and her siblings had all married and moved away. "When we came back, everything had changed. The slower-paced days were gone." Disney had come to town! Orange and Seminole counties were growing. Sanlando Springs Tropical Park had been sold to Earl Downs who was busy developing a new community: The Springs.

Over lunch at the home of *Mayanne Downs,* stories unfolded of her father, real estate developer Earl Downs. Through community planning and construction, Downs Properties played a role in transforming mid-century Orlando with landmark projects. Earl Downs transformed more than the landscape; he made decisions based on a desire to protect the environment, and by reflecting on how we live with each other in our environment. Mayanne recalled one of her father's memorable projects. "My Dad built one of the first real office buildings in Orlando." Construction on Summerlin Center began in 1961 at the corner of South Street and Summerlin Avenue. Downs was granted a loan based on a pre-leased occupancy rate of 25%. The building would predominantly house medical offices. The Southern Building Code at the time required racially segregated waiting areas. The Downs family was deeply devoted to the civil rights movement. In good conscience, Earl could not build within those segregationist codes. All pre-leased doctors agreed to the single waiting room office design. When the city's construction inspectors reviewed the site, once the drywall was up, they could plainly see there were no walls dividing the waiting rooms. The inspectors red-tagged the project, shutting down construction, but Downs would not budge. The building site was ghostly quiet for 48 hours. Then, with no fanfare, the tags were removed. The city of Orlando was given the gentle nudge needed to turn the page on an ugly part of history. Mayanne remembers her father later reflecting on this footnote in his career. "The commissioners decided this wasn't a fight they wanted to have. They recognized that a change was needed and they weren't going to stand in the way of that change."

LIFE ALONG THE LITTLE WEKIVA

Earl Downs viewed the world, and therefore his projects, with social responsibility. He searched for ways to make an impact on his community in order to make life better for those who lived in it. With this framework, he approached an interesting development idea for the property surrounding Sanlando Springs. His wife, Sally Shearouse, grew up in Orlando. The Shearouse family was deeply rooted in the city. Five-year-old Sally even represented the City Beautiful as Little Miss Orlando! As a young girl, she swam at Sanlando Springs, enjoying all the wonders the park had to offer. Earl, who was originally from Birmingham, Alabama, discovered this iconic Central Florida playground through Sally's happy memories.

Shortly after the Korean War, Earl, an Air Force veteran, was picking up a military prisoner at the Pine Castle Air Force Base in Orlando. It was that glorious time of the year when orange blossoms perfumed the air. When he stepped out of the transport vehicle, his first deep breath, laced with the intoxicating scent, filled him with a sense of happiness. "I gotta live here!" And that's just what he did. Not long after, he met the lovely Sally. She was one of eight young women in the University of Florida's first coed graduating class. Intelligent, with an adventurous, sparkling personality, Sally helped Earl set down roots in Central Florida. The couple and their growing family made a home among the orange groves.

Sanlando Tropical Park 1947s
(State Library and Archives of Florida)

When Sally introduced Earl and the children to the tropical paradise surrounding Sanlando Springs, she regaled them with stories of summer evening dances, walks through the gardens, long slides, and big dives into the crystal-clear waters of the spring. Mayanne, her sisters, and brother made their own memories at the park, but Mayanne's memories of the iconic slide are more of a "one and done" experience. "I went down the tall *slide o-scratch* once, and that was enough." Earl, on the other hand, thought it all was "enchanting."

Mayanne laughed as she shared her perspective on the ideas forming in her Dad's mind—"he was always the entrepreneur," envisioning all sorts of possibilities for the beautiful spot that generations of Central Florida residents had come to love. He could see unique opportunities for creating an innovative living experience. Plans continued to percolate. In 1970, with J.E. Robinson's management of Sanlando

Springs Tropical Park coming to an end, the time was right to turn ideas into reality.

By this time, Downs had formed Epoch Properties. Jim Pugh and John McClintock worked with him. Epoch was focused on the new trend of multi-family communities.²⁹ The property around the springs provided an intriguing opportunity to take this idea to the next level. Plans developed, that included a diverse collection of neighborhoods within the larger community. There would be several amenities, including central gardens spread out around the spring, stables for equestrians to board their horses, a spa, and pools.

Downs succeeded in negotiating a land lease from the Overstreet Land Co., but he also needed to acquire several privately held parcels. There were small landholders with campsites scattered along the Little Wekiva River. Downs had his hands full making all the individual deals necessary for Epoch to move forward with the land they needed. With 400 acres secured, the next step was to meet with county commissioners about their vision for the development. The land around Sanlando Springs was publicly zoned as a park, so Downs worked closely with Seminole County on zoning issues. Commissioners were not happy about losing a unique community asset, but Downs's excitement for the project and his conservationist mindset eventually put the zoning board at ease.

Downs and Pugh were able to continue to let their imaginations run wild with plans for the development. Jim Pugh once told me when we spoke briefly several years ago that during those early years, planning the neighborhood had been a lot of fun. "We had go-carts and we'd run them around Springs Boulevard. It was just a dirt road then." They were laying plans for the "villages" and the rest of the community as they tooled around in their carts.

Earl Downs at The Springs, 1970s (Mayanne Downs)

The *Orlando Sentinel*, in a 1994 article highlighting Epoch's mark on Orlando, stated: "The Springs was the first planned unit development approved by the county."²⁹ Defining characteristics of planned unit developments include private amenities for residents and homeowners associations, which set guidelines for building design. Downs envisioned people living and playing together. He intended for single homeowners and first time buyers to have access to the same amenities that those in a higher income bracket enjoyed. A clubhouse would be centered near Sanlando Springs with a racquet club, basketball courts, and pools nearby. Horse stables and a storage facility for members' boats and RVs were included in the design. All these amenities provided residents with unique benefits that few neighborhoods built at the time offered.

Condominiums, townhouses, mid-sized homes, and large sprawling estates all mingled together along winding roads that curved through the woods. This was, and still is, in stark contrast to many developments that clear-cut the land and arrange similarly designed homes in a box-like grid. The homes were loosely organized into 20 villages with idyllic names like Whispering Pines and Glenwood Village. Each village would have their own governance within the larger homeowner's association. The renowned Florida architect Nils M. Schweizer worked with Downs and the Epoch team. Schweizer focused on mid-century modern architecture, and his work in The Springs exemplified these principles.[30]

Mayanne pointed out other defining characteristics of The Springs. "There would be no curbs. This was an environmental feature. Run-off from the streets would percolate naturally," instead of

being channeled into a rush of water that would funnel into gutters and end up flushing into the river basin. The community was designed with extensive green space so water could seep into the aquifers. This lack of curbing also kept everything looking more natural. The meandering roads were less defined, giving a relaxed, natural feel to the place. Native plants were the stars. When additional landscaping was needed, the team was intentional about not planting hedges that would require intense watering and pruning. Then there were the trees! Thanks to Epochs conservationist approach, towering pines and old oaks stand proudly. Their branches stretch wide, like arms reaching out to wrap you in a loving embrace. "Trees were a big deal to my Dad. The development first and foremost was planned around the trees."

Reflecting on the community, Mayanne said, "My Dad was really proud of the work he did in The Springs. He was proud of the houses he built. He loved that people would live their lives in them. They'd celebrate triumphs and share trials around the dinner table. Conflicts and resolutions would be made. Building homes provided a place for all of that. This made him happy."

The Downs family believed in the value of this new venture so much that they built their own home along the river. A TV advertisement promoting the new development exclaimed, *"Doctors Live in The Springs, Engineers Live in The Springs, Even the Developer of The Springs Lives in The Springs."* The Downs family moved from their beloved orange grove to the new development before it officially opened. The power and water weren't even on yet! It was a grand adventure for the family. They showered at the clubhouse pool for about a month. Their first home was a townhouse in one of the villages. Eventually, they moved to a beautiful home by the Little Wekiva on Riverbend Drive. The family loved the idea that they could technically walk out their backdoor, set out in a boat, and float to the Atlantic Ocean.

The description of The Springs on neighborhoods.com captures the essence of this special community just as Earl Downs and Jim Pugh envisioned it.

> "At Home With Nature" is The Springs's slogan. The neighborhood is "teeming with flora and fauna. It's common to find trees well over a hundred years old and all sorts of active wildlife along the banks of the Little Wekiva River. Living in The Springs, it's easy to forget that all the modern, urban conveniences are right outside the community."[31]

The focus of the community revolves around nature and the spring waters flowing among them. The magic surrounding Sanlando Springs continues, it's just wrapped up in a different package. Yet another generation is enjoying the Little Wekiva River, the springs, and the land surrounding them.

Little Wekiva Memories

John Rountree and I sat together under one of the ancient oak trees near the edge of Sanlando Springs. "When I was just a boy, back in the 50s and 60s, we'd pay 25 cents admission, and that would get us into the park." Sweeping his arms up toward a grassy area just beyond the spring, he said, "There was a hotdog stand right over there, a rope swing down there near the gazebo, and a 30 foot slide that dropped us into the water." What's not to love about that if you're a kid? As he gazed across the still waters of the spring, he said, "this place holds a special place in my heart."

John's parents moved to College Park when he was 6 months old. "Dad worked in Orlando as a district supervisor and fruit inspector. Orlando was a quiet town in the those days. There were orange groves spread all over this area." John's grandparents grew grapefruit and oranges. The family business was based in Frostproof, Florida, near Lake Wales. Frostproof was a major citrus-producing area in Florida. The town carried an ironic name given that it was hit with several devastating freezes in the late 1800s, early 1900s, and again in the late 1980s. John spent his summers working for his grandparents in the groves, then back to College Park for school in the fall. He eventually graduated from Edgewater High School, developing an interest in tennis.

Life brings twists and turns that we could never predict or plan. One of those surprising twists in John's life was spending over 30 idyllic years as the Tennis Pro of The Springs Racket Club.

In 1990, after high pressure positions in Japan and at the Orlando Tennis and Racket Club, John accepted the offer to come to The Springs. From sun-drenched childhood days, splashing in the refreshing water of Sanlando Springs, to managing a thriving racket club a few hundred feet from that same spring, John enjoyed a sweet full-circle experience. He found the pace at The Springs Racket Club relaxing after the big clubs he'd been working at. "When I came to work at The Springs Racket Club, I felt like I was home. I had so many happy memories there as a kid that, coming back, I felt like I belonged. I appreciated the beauty and the unique surroundings. Places like this are rare; they're worth protecting. It was such a peaceful place to work."

The courts and clubhouse are nestled in the trees. Sanlando Springs is just a short walk away, and happy voices of children playing in the water can be heard on the courts. A boardwalk ends at the far side of the club, connecting residents from all over the community who have taken a short-cut across a little bridge spanning the Little Wekiva to come and play at the racket club.

It was important to John to help people learn to love the game of tennis. He found great joy in teaching. All three of our children took lessons from John. His commitment to the club helped foster the sense of community that is so iconic at The Springs. He valued the friendships that formed on the courts. Beyond building relationships and helping people grow skills and a love for the game, John organized schedules, planned community leagues, and took care of the facilities.

This included preparing for hurricanes which always bring flooding to the low-lying area near the racket club. The river rises, and water flows right across the courts. Another storm that stands out in John's memory was a rare hailstorm in the early 2000s. He remembers the day clearly. "I closed the club early and tried to beat it home. Hail started falling so quickly that I was blinded in a whiteout of ice covering the ground. It was difficult for me to navigate. I couldn't see the road. Driving up the hill from the tennis courts, I couldn't tell where the lawns began or where the road ended."

It is more common to battle the blazing Florida sun. The warmth brings out alligators, who like to soak up the rays. "For a while there was a gator that liked to sun himself right by the gate to the tennis courts." One evening, this big fellow held John hostage. From the safe side of the fence, John called out insults and rattled the fence until the alligator decided to move along.

LIFE ALONG THE LITTLE WEKIVA

You never know what animal will pop by for a visit at The Springs Racket Club. During heavy rains, when the springs overflow and run through the woods around the courts, otters have been seen swimming near the fence. The bears, who consider The Springs their stomping ground, have been spotted in the trees nearby with their cubs. Deer are so comfortable, they barely notice as people walk by with rackets in hand.

The menagerie of animals that stop by for a visit, couples walking hand in hand down the boardwalk on their way back home after a swim in the spring, families picnicking by the water—these are scenes that John grew to love during his time at The Springs Racket Club. John appreciated the distinct way life was lived at the community. "Life was centered around the spring and people wanted a more laid back lifestyle."

John's first customer at the racket club back in 1990 was Gill Newkirk. He was a frequent tennis player who became a great friend. Gill was also the final guest on John's last day at the club in 2022. A perfect bookend to a career devoted to that distinct way of life in The Springs.

The Springs Racket Club is in transition. The pickleball craze has hit The Springs just as it has across the country. Pickle-ballers share space with the die-hard tennis players. Recent hurricanes have taken their toll on the courts, but there are high hopes for bringing The Springs Racket Club back to its former glory. The racket club represents much more than just a place to hit a few balls. The club is a key ingredient in the special mix of amenities that make The Springs a standout community.

Ron and Lisa Huston have lived in The Springs since 1987. They were drawn to the neighborhood because they fell in love with its wild, natural environment. Homes were required by the HOA to have a natural color palette so they blended into their wooded surroundings. As the development grew, Lisa said it was like "houses were just dropped in the woods." Despite development, wildlife felt at home. Residents learned to coexist with their animal neighbors. Ron and Lisa's home is in the back of the neighborhood, near the Little Wekiva River and Starbuck Spring. They felt like they were living in paradise.

Ron makes friends easily. He shares colorful stories involving wild Florida: its turkeys, bears, snakes, and armadillos. Ron even has a tale to tell about armadillos and leprosy! Another story paints a funny picture of him returning home, to find a bear playing in their swimming pool. Through the years, he's had conversations with some of the characters that have played a part in the history of the springs on the Little Wekiva. His tales help us imagine what the area was like before development and help us get to know the people who dotted the landscape a bit better by painting a fuller picture of their experiences.

Shortly after moving into The Springs, Ron remembers a conversation with his neighbor, Lloyd Latshaw. Latshaw and Guy Rizzo were golfing buddies. In the mid 1980s, while playing a round of golf, Latshaw convinced Rizzo to sell him his undeveloped land along the Little Wekiva. The wild beauty of the property was captivating, but Rizzo felt the time was right to dispose of the property, so he agreed to sell the parcel to Latshaw for what he had purchased it for a few years before. Guy Rizzo recalled the adventures he and his bother-in-law had trying to beat back the jungle. They spent time trying to keep an area clear so his family could enjoy the river. However, in the absence of regular human presence, wildlife claimed the land for their own. While mowing through weeds growing around the trees, they startled a large snake. The snake dropped on the mower, sending Guy's brother-in-law running. This is property that our family would later own. Today, when Jeff, my husband, goes out to mow, the hawks perch on low hanging branches waiting for snakes and other creatures that are stirred by the noise.

Thicket near spring

Landscape near spring

Another river story involves Don Barker. Ron remembers being told that Don met a local man during his time flying with the Civilian Pilot Training Program in Florida during WWII. While flying over the Little Wekiva tributary, he was caught up in the beauty of Sanlando Springs. The spring was an oasis amidst a thick growth of trees and underbrush covering the area. It all looked so magical from the sky. Then, like a hidden gem emerging, he saw another dot of turquoise peeking out of the dense greenery. He was surprised to discover this smaller spring tucked in the woods. Once on the ground, it didn't take Don long to pack a bag for exploration. He and a friend set off on a motorbike, cutting their way through thick jungle, guided only by a compass. The men finally found the spring in the wild woods. Emerging from the thicket, Don stood in front of a beautiful, bubbling spring flowing through the trees. The landscape looked otherworldly. He was overcome by a desire to call this bit of paradise his own.

Searching property records, he discovered who owned the surrounding acreage. Shephard Spring, which was eventually renamed Starbuck Spring, after Starbuck Yale, became a retreat for the Yale and Barker families. It was their weekend escape from the "city" of Orlando.

When asked to describe what it's like to live in The Springs, Lisa describes an idyllic scene. "We used to see people on horseback all the time." Stables are a part of the community plan. Owners can board their horses and ride the trails along the river.

"It's such a laid back, family place. The community used to host a Halloween party at the clubhouse over by the spring, complete with a haunted house." Traditions like the Easter Egg Hunt, started by the Overstreets when they owned and ran Sanlando Springs as a community park, have continued in some form or another. Santa Claus still makes an appearance at the annual Christmas parade. Luminaries line Springs Boulevard. Hot chocolate stands pop up around the route inviting neighbors to come together and celebrate. Lisa remembers, "kids used to ride go-carts around the loop." A tradition started by Jim Pugh perhaps? Safety concerns have put a stop to kids flying around the loop on go-carts, but

Easter Egg Hunt (Overstreet)

Sanlando Springs—ladies posing on bridge over north run (State Library and Archives of Florida)

the neighborhood is still full of families riding bikes, walking their dogs, or going for a run. You'll often see people with towels slung around their necks, and beach chairs strapped to their backs heading to the spring for a swim. Chances are high that you'll run into deer grazing among the trees, peacocks shrieking from a perch in tall pines, or raccoons darting across the grass.

Lisa shared several vintage pictures of Sanlando Springs Tropical Park. In its heyday, the park drew people from the area who came to soak up the sun and rest in the shade of the huge trees surrounding the spring. Looking at pictures with Lisa, highlighting scenes from Sanlando's past, it's hard not to feel a sense of romance for those days. Living here today is like having a link to that past.

Ron's mother, Miriam Oestricher, recalls the springs before it was The Springs. "My Dad would get us all together and take us to Sanlando Springs. It was a jaunt for us to get up there." The family lived in the College Park area, near what is now AdventHealth's flagship Orlando campus. "The hospital was just a small wooden building then." Miriam remembers playing in the woods and running through orange groves near Lakes Estelle and Ivanhoe. "We had bamboo fishing rods hidden behind trees near all the lakes so, wherever we went, we could grab our poles and fish." Growing up with freedom to roam and forests to explore was grand, but a trip to Sanlando Springs was something extra special. "We didn't go that often. It was a big deal." Driving on the dirt roads made the relatively short distance seem much longer and more arduous. Once they arrived, they would go straight to the changing area to put on their bathing suits. There were lockers to store their things, and the locker keys were kept on an elastic band that they'd slip around their ankles. Then they were off, running across the lawn, anticipating their splash in the cool spring after the long, hot drive.

Visits to Sanlando Springs were so memorable that, when talking to people decades later, their recollections are still vivid. Stories unfold easily as if it all happened yesterday. This was certainly the case with Miriam. "There was a stainless steel 'elephant' chained to the limestone bottom." The steel drum was a challenge for people to keep their balance on. It gave everyone who accepted the challenge a real workout. "If you could get up on it, it was hard to stay on." Miriam fiercely stated, "I was determined to get up on that thing, but it was slimy. We all just slid right back off!"

Playing on the elephant 1946 (State Library and Archives of Florida)

Several years ago Miriam met a man named Carl Baratta who was a citrus grower in the Orlando area. His stories give us another picture of what life used to be like on the Little Wekiva River. He remembers the wide, fast moving, river being used to run logs. The logging industry was thriving in the early 1900s. The foundations of old sawmills near the springs hint at the past and stir the imagination. If we close our eyes, and let our mind's eye take over, we can see loggers with long poles jumping from log to log as they direct the flow of pines down the river on their way to Sanford and Lake Monroe and finally, the St. Johns River.

Miriam seemed to get a little wistful as she reflected on the changes along the river, its springs, and the lakes. "Everything was nature. It was calmer and quieter." When Interstate 4 came through Orlando in the 1960s, the family orange groves were cut in half to make way for the highway. A few years later, Sanlando Springs Tropical Park closed its doors. The Springs community, while honoring its natural surroundings, nonetheless brought drastic changes to the landscape. This in turn, spurred other development in the area. Central Florida was growing by leaps and bounds.

Logging on the Wekiva River 1890s (Florida Library and State Archives)

When Ron and Lisa were newly married, a bank-owned property became available in The Springs. With nostalgic stories from Ron's mother nudging them forward, the couple dove into the project of renovating a house, and making The Springs their home. Their family adventures on this stretch of the Little Wekiva River in Longwood sound similar to stories shared by others from long ago. They hunt for turtles near Palm Springs and explore the jungle around Ginger Ale Springs. With full-throttled dives, they land in the cool, clear water of Sanlando Springs. Together with friends, they relax by the water's edge, enjoying the tranquility that comes with time spent in nature.

Huston's adventures (Huston Family)

Orlando Philharmonic Pops Concert at The Springs (Huston family)

Another favorite pastime enjoyed at The Springs is the annual Orlando Philharmonic Pops Concert. This outdoor event, staged by the water, continues the tradition of reveling in music at Sanlando Springs. Residents and visitors from the community set up their chairs on the lawn, not far from the old dance floor. Music drifting from speakers, hung from the trees in the 1930s to the harmonies of the orchestra almost a hundred years later—the rhythms continue at Sanlando Springs. For people longing to enjoy the beauty of the spring and relive memories from their childhood, when the park was open to the public, this is a wonderful opportunity to do just that! As in years past, you can purchase tickets to come bask in the music under the stars by the spring.

Billy Ridgeback Bodie was looking forward to another great day, hanging out with friends on the beach by Sanlando Springs. It was a beautiful March morning. I walked over to the spring to meet Billy. He'd agreed to share some of his memories about growing up in The Springs. As we talked, the beach area was filling up. Billy would nod and wave as familiar faces set up their beach chairs nearby. A feeling of "the gang's all here" was taking over.

We sat down at a picnic table in the sun. Billy looked out over the still water. He thought quietly for a moment, before he began sharing his thoughts. He shook his head, stretched out his arms, and almost with disbelief, said, "it was all orange groves and pine trees." He seemed amazed by how quickly it all had changed. Thinking back to when he was just a boy, Billy shared his story and his connection to this special spot on the Little Wekiva River.

LITTLE WEKIVA MEMORIES

Soft-shell turtles

Billy was born in Maitland, the youngest of eight siblings. Their parents used to take them to swim at Sanlando Springs Tropical Park, paying just 25 cents for admission. A move to California ended their family outings to the springs. During their time away, the park had been sold, and development began on The Springs. When the family returned to Central Florida in 1977, they moved into this new community. They were glad to be a part of the unique neighborhood that was intent on preserving a bit of Florida's wild beauty. By this time, Billy was the only child left at home. Happy memories of swimming at Sanlando Springs Tropical Park with his brothers and sisters were tucked in the back of his mind, but now it was time to make his own memories.

He remembered that there was a spring near the river, so he and a friend went on the hunt to rediscover it. "We were free spirits, digging and exploring through the wild woods," recalls Billy. They discovered a small turquoise swimming hole. Thinking they had found "THE" spring, the boys returned there often to play. It was a secluded, untamed area, just right for boys who wanted to wile away afternoons fishing for bass and catfish. They got pretty good at catching snakes too. Hog nose, indigos, along with rat snakes and water moccasins were frequently seen. Billy remembers that in the 70s and 80s, it was not uncommon to see eight foot snakes lurking in the undergrowth.

The boys also followed soft shell turtles as they swam in the waters. Billy estimates they were three to four feet in diameter. Billy and his friends jumped from rope swings left hanging from trees over the river. They pretended they were Tarzan, just as movie heroes had done in those same waters in the 1960s. Billy also recalls playing around a large abandoned hotel. The ruins were most likely what remained of Haithcox's grand plans when he ran the springs area as a park and vacation spot in the mid 1920s. The structure gave the boys a backdrop for great adventures. Wild Florida with its constant, creeping growth was doing a good job of hiding the foundations from most people, but not from the eyes of curious boys.

Sanlando Springs, 1960s (State Library and Archives of Florida)

It wasn't long before Billy met another boy in the neighborhood who asked him if he wanted to go swim in the spring with him. It was a big surprise for Billy when they ended up at a huge spring, not the small deserted one he'd been playing at. He was amazed by Sanlando's wide sandy beach, the expanse of grass sloping toward the water, the big, beautiful trees, and clumps of tall palms. Kids played on floats in the water. Billy and his friend determined to keep their other hideaway a secret. Of course, it wasn't a secret to the Barker family who owned the several acres surrounding Starbuck Spring where the boys had been playing before their discovery of Sanlando Springs.

In the 70s, when Billy's family moved into The Springs, the trees were more dense than they are today. He recalls that the homes were intentionally built from cedar so they would blend into their surroundings. "In the early days, while the development was being built, there was a wood mill that was in constant use, preparing boards for use in construction." The homes were rising up among the trees. Nature paths were tucked in the woods near the river. Seeing people on horseback along the paths was common.

When driving into The Springs, Billy feels like a weight is being lifted off his shoulders. "Living here is a big stress reliever." He describes the community as perfectly secluded, but so close to everything that's right outside the gates. As we talked, I could easily understand why Billy and his friends live for their relaxing weekend barbecues by the spring. They cherish traditions that have been celebrated for centuries. Hanging out on the beach is a throwback to those simpler days. Time slows dow a bit. Reflecting on his childhood, Billy said, "this place can shape your life in positive ways. Kids spend more time outdoors. Families relax and play together. The environment encourages people to take advantage of all the sun, sand, water, and wildlife." The Little Wekiva River and the springs that flow into it can do a lot to restore you— if you'll just keep yourself open to experiencing what they have to offer. As Billy watched kids splashing in the water, he added, "it's a great place to grow up—a great place to raise a family. It's a place you'll never want to leave."

LIFE ALONG THE LITTLE WEKIVA

Painting of spring with bird

Our conversation was also tinged with a bit of sadness. Billy remembers when the gates, or weirs, placed on either end of the spring were regularly controlled, allowing water in the spring to build up and self clean before spilling back into the river. Like others I've talked to, Billy has noticed a change in the health of the water. Continued area development takes its toll on the environment. Areas like Cranes Roost, in Altamonte Springs, release water into the river when their lake level is high. "The city could pump excess water through a 1.6-mile force main into the Little Wekiva River."[27] This runoff water ends up flooding the springs. When this happens, Sanlando Springs is closed until the water clears again. Billy has noticed that this happens more frequently now and it takes longer to clear. "The water just isn't as clean as it used to be."

We need to take care of our waterways, springs and aquifers. They are the lifeblood of Florida. Organizations like *Friends of the Wekiva* host clean-up days on the river. We can join their efforts, but we can also jump in and do our part by paying attention to how we live along our oceans, rivers, lakes, and springs. After heavy storms, log jams build up collecting all sorts of debris. Leif and his Dad have pulled surprising bits of garbage from those jams: balls of every size and variety, old cans and bottles, shoes, etc., anything you discard carelessly, it likely will end up in the river. With watchful care, we can work together as a team, ensuring that our rivers stay clean and beautiful for generations to come.

Parker Wilson has spent 30 years caring for Central Florida's waterways. He knows the St. Johns River and the Wekiva River Basin inside and out. Parker and his crew have done all manner of clearing, taming, rebuilding, and adventuring along the river. Until his retirement, he was always ready to help with storm cleanups and was equipped to expertly handle the toughest jobs Florida's jungle could throw at you. Parker is a great story teller. His tales are full of adventures set in the wild landscape he calls home.

Parker's main contributions to Sanlando Springs and the Little Wekiva started in the early 2000s. He was contacted by a friend, Bob Kane, who was a board member at The Springs. The community used to be self governed, with a board of citizens volunteering and a longtime staff running the offices. Kane was concerned that the beloved spring, the center piece—the heartbeat of the community—was becoming overgrown. The water clarity was not what it once was. He desperately wanted to help keep the spring healthy, but this was no

South run area clean up and tree stump removed from south run (Parker Wilson)

small job. The spring runs flowing into the Little Wekiva River were clogged, and the flow of water into the river had become more of a trickle. Overflow from Sanlando's boil was seeping into the jungle thickets instead of running through a defined waterway. Heavy rains would cause the river and spring to flow together. Without a clear run, the spring water mixing with river water and unwanted plant life was tainting the naturally clean water from the aquifer. Invasive plants were starting to grow in Sanlando Springs. Parker and his team came in and dredged the spring's south run. They carefully beat back the jungle to work their way to the overgrown pump house. A huge tree had fallen in the marshy area. Upon removing the stump, they found it had settled into a sand boil, blocking the spring water's flow from there as well. Once the jungle was cut back a bit, several small boils were discovered bubbling up in the south run of Sanlando Springs.

Parker continued to help repair and replace walls and equipment in order to ensure the spring would run clear without debris clogging the flow. The north run was cleared in the spring of 2002. Parker replaced weirs that had deteriorated, thereby ensuring that the spring water could be controlled, creating a beautiful, usable swimming area. It had been 30 years since Sanlando Springs Tropical Park had closed. The work around the spring that was done when Earl Downs laid out The Springs was in need of maintenance to ensure that the community could continue to enjoy the remarkable natural wonder in their midst. Parker worked with the company Specialty Marine Contractors, which built a wall that supported one side of the spring's south run. Mike, with Specialty Marine, built a wooden arch bridge over the south run. Partnership with R&R Concrete laid new sidewalks and a retaining wall along the grassy slopes. The existing walls surrounding the spring had begun to crumble. The new walls cover the original ones, giving them a much needed facelift and extra support.

The beach area was also cleaned. Parker remembers that neighbors would come help with cleanup around the springs, working along with him and his team. Parker and Bob Kane spent many evenings planting 6 ft palms around the beach. These palms have now grown into stately landmarks. Their shadows flitter across the sand and their reflections dance on the water.

Parker and others used to call Palm Springs, the "Lost Spring," because not too long ago that is exactly what it was. "People didn't even know it was there," recalls Parker. "Even though it was right off of a cul-de-sac, a short walk from Sanlando, it was completely hidden behind thick brush and trees. You could barely get through the brush to see the water."

Helping to clean up around Palm Springs and Sanlando Springs was a rewarding experience for Parker. He felt great satisfaction as progress was made to clear the water, restore the common areas surrounding the springs, and trim back overgrowth. Part of his joy came from the connection he felt to Sanlando Springs. He remembers playing there as a child. Like so many others who grew up in Central Florida before "progress" changed the landscape, he and his family followed dirt roads to Sanlando Springs. They paid their 25 cents for admission which gave them access to a magical world, filled with adventure. Parker recalls renting a canoe with his friends. Each trip up the river would bring surprises. Hawks perched in trees—ready to dive for a snake or wood mouse that might stir in the grass. Gar fish darted under their canoes. There was a quiet beauty to the landscape. These moments settled in their head and hearts, creating memories that have lasted a lifetime.

Big Slide, 1930s (Rick Kilby)

Boys jumping into pool (Overstreet)

Parker's memories are shared by a generation of Central Florida residents. It was common for area schools to visit Sanlando Springs for field trips. Parker laughed, "if you could jump into one end of the big cement pool and swim to the other side, you "passed" and you could go swim in the spring." The big slide and diving board were, of course, favorite highlights.

Robert Brinton is a good friend of Parker's. He knows how to make quick work of an after-storm clean up. Robert cared for the trees in The Springs for many years. He remembers trees so thick along Springs Boulevard that the houses were completely lost in the leaves. While there are an abundance of trees in The Springs today, houses aren't hidden as they once were. Hurricanes and lack of replanting have taken their toll. There have been subtle changes to the look of The Springs.

LIFE ALONG THE LITTLE WEKIVA

It's inevitable, that as the landscape of Central Florida has changed drastically over the last 50 years, change would occur within the gates of The Springs as well. As the years go by, new generations of residents who move into The Springs aren't always aware of its unique history. Parker shared some things he's learned through the years as he's spent time on the Little Wekiva River and around the springs that flow into it. "It's important to be careful when working in springs so you don't damage or break the limestone floor. It's best to clean the springs by hand like they do at Wekiva Springs State Park." He went on to say that, "All waterways boil down to runoff. What ends up in our rivers, springs, lakes, and the whole St Johns River basin is what we dump into our environment." If we can ensure a healthy runoff by diminishing hazardous fertilizers and cleaning up our waste, we can help keep our waterways clean. Each one of us is responsible. What we do today creates the world for future generations.

The Springs Community continues its work maintaining the natural wonder in their midst, recognizing that they are today's caretakers and preservationists for the next generation. In 2022 a major waterfront revitalization plan was set in motion. The Springs Community, with assistance from Habitat Restoration and Wildlife Protection Services, works within guidelines set by the St. Johns River Water Management District, U.S. Army Corps of Engineers, and the Florida Department of Environmental Protection. Together, the goal is to address issues caused by fertilizers that find their way into the river and spring water, causing unsightly algae and plant blooms. A dredging project will remove sand and soil that have settled on top of the limerock in Sanlando Springs. Berms, with native plants, grasses, and flowers will be added around the spring to protect the water from runoff and flooding. Projects like these take time and money. I feel grateful to those who carry on the tradition of taking care of the Little Wekiva River and the springs that flow into it.

South run of Sanlando Springs

LIFE ALONG THE LITTLE WEKIVA

Our family moved to The Springs in 2009. We were amazed at the wildlife all around us. Our daughter, Juliet, started keeping a list of the creatures she was seeing. The drive through the neighborhood would often stall as we waited for wildlife to cross the road. Guineafowls waddled by, their dark, football-shaped bodies boasting a spray of tiny white speckles. Occasionally, a fox would dart through the trees. Juliet's list grew so quickly that it was hard to keep up. The list-making was set aside, and enjoyment and wonder took over. Zoos lost their allure. We lived in a zoo without fences. We saw wild animals in their natural environment every time we stepped outside. The bears were so plentiful we began to take their presence for granted. It's not uncommon to take a turn in the road and see a bear lumbering right down the middle of the lane. We've had walks interrupted as bears cross the street in front of us. A volleyball game in the backyard was frozen in mid-play as a bear emerged from the woods. We all stood still, watching intently as he walked by, totally uninterested in us. He ambled across our bridge, crossing the Little Wekiva and moving into the woods. Not too long after that memorable volleyball game, we installed a motion camera on a tree near the waters edge. We discovered that all sorts of wild life use the same path that the bear had taken. Coming from a thicket near the water, they head across the bridge, then along the shore toward the tree line on the far side of our small island. The island divides Starbuck Spring Run and the riverbed. This is where the berries are—a big draw for bears! Frequently, a raccoon family would tumble out of the woods, following each other across that bridge. Armadillos roam. Coyotes howl and dart across this animal overpass. Big water birds come in for a landing by the river. Eagles swoop down. Alligators sun themselves when they think no one else is around. And then of course, there are more bears.

(Sue Tyndall)

On a hot summer day, the kids and I, and a few friends were working in the creek with my friend Sue. Intent on our work, our heads were down. All of a sudden, Devin dashed by me. I turned to see him standing twenty feet away, pointing back across the creek. Following his gaze, I turned back and looked up the bank. A big bear was looking down on me. He seemed pretty unconcerned by all of us. His attitude was in sharp contrast to ours. We all slowly backed away from him and stood with Devin a good distance away. Sue, on the other hand, stood her ground and talked to the burly bear as he walked off in search of berries.

This was not the only time she had dealt with local bears. By this time Sue had moved to a different neighborhood within The Springs. I hopped on my bike to ride over for a visit. Sitting in her living room by a big picture window that looked out into a wooded area, we talked about the wildlife that came by her window. She joyfully recalled the time a curious little bear wobbled over to her window, stood up on his hind legs, and leaned in for a look. There she was—face to face with a bear—the glass being the only thing separately her from the cutie just inches away.

Every so often, while kayaking up the river, we see turtles sunning on logs stretched across the water. They always bring a smile to our faces. Sometimes, we'll hear a splash and turn toward the noise in time to see the turtle's tail end slipping into the water. Friends who live on the river often see a giant turtle that swims in the spring. They estimate that he looks to be well over 5o lbs. Leif and I were lucky to see a strangely beautiful, soft shell turtle swimming in the south run of Sanlando Springs.

The Little Wekiva River continues to share its wonderful surprises. Today, the water is very clear, with mostly spring water running through. As I write, hurricane season is bearing down on us. The spring-fed creek will turn into a lake for a while, stealing some of our yard. A tangle of debris will lodge against the braces of our bridge. Soon, the intense period of time when plants grow wild will slow and the weather will cool, allowing our family to spend more time relaxing by the water's edge.

We join generations of people who have gone before us, finding rest and rejuvenation in the cool waters of the springs. Our family has found the Little Wekiva River to be intriguing. We find our way to river's edge when we need to escape. It is easy to get lost in thought as you float down the river while dragonflies dart about.

Curious otters trail our kayaks. Being on the river is like being on a treasure hunt. What surprise awaits around the next bend? Will I get to see a fresh water ray today? Will there be a snake sunning on the bank, coiled around knobby knees of a cypress tree? It is a thrill finding the "big one" while hunting for shark teeth. It is pretty cool to watch as long, narrow, gar fish slip beneath our kayaks. Seeing a stream of clear water we've never noticed before, emptying into the river, brings questions to mind. What boil is the water escaping from? Have we found a new spring run? All this fills our minds, pushing the stress, concerns, and responsibilities of our busy lives far away for a while.

LIFE ALONG THE LITTLE WEKIVA

... All this—while we're on the river.

Sometimes Jeff will come bursting into the house after a long day of work. In a matter of minutes, he's roaring out the back door, hopping on his mower, where he spends an hour in the backyard. With each methodical pass of the mower, Jeff wipes away the burdens of his day.

"Henry" the Hawk—as the kids have named him—perches on a low-hanging branch while Jeff is busy in the yard. Henry wisely stands at the ready to swoop down and grab in his talons the snakes and other small creatures Jeff stirs with his mover.

Early one recent morning, while it was still cool, I set out for a walk. I followed the meandering streets that were so thoughtfully laid out by Earl Downs and Jim Pugh. Large trees stretched toward the sky. Stately pines with long, straight trunks burst into a flurry of pine needle bouquets. As I walked, I noticed delicate scratching sounds. I stopped, looked up, and saw a little bird clinging to the trunk's scaly bark. Then I saw a squirrel darting across a branch further up. As he ran along nimbly, little clicking noises floated through the air as his claws grabbed the bark. Pausing, I noticed another squirrel, and then another. The chase was on. They scurried round and round the trunk, in and out of pine needle clusters, causing small helicopter-like seeds to swirl into a beautiful earthbound descent.

While walking the winding path that follows Springs Boulevard, there is evidence of actual fairies in our midst. Here and there, tucked into gnarled holes at the base of tree trunks, tiny cottages and whimsical scenes dot the landscape. In Glenwood's Fairy Forest, hidden among the magnolias, heavy-laden with their large, milky-white flowers, these hints of otherworldliness send one's mind to imaginary places where gnomes and their friends might actually take up residence. In the tree tops, squirrels leap from branch to large palm fronds, that spring like a trampoline under their weight. Peacocks call out in delight. What a magical place to live!

Glenwood's Fairy Forest

Living in The Springs encourages you to be mindful of nature. It engages your senses. There is always something that tempts you to stop, relax, and appreciate the gifts we've been given. If you have not been on a river in Florida, played in one of her springs, kayaked the intercostal waterways, or explored Florida's wild tropical forests, Leif and I encourage you to get out there! You will not be disappointed. It is a world like no other. When so much of our daily lives are organized, computerized, and digitized, it is refreshing to get outside and discover the peace that comes from being on the river. Adventure Awaits.

Florida's natural springs will welcome you into their cool, clean pools.

Will you let the springs work their magic on you?

Do you hear the river calling?

Answer that call.

We know you will enjoy the journey.

LITTLE WEKIVA MEMORIES

While sitting on the porch at their camp by the Little Wekiva River, reveling in the beauty all around her, Sarah Overstreet penned these lines.

Reflections on her favorite place to be:
The time would be a springtime day
The place a wooded dell
The earth a carpet deep with moss
Where scattered sunlight fell.

The sky I scarce could see above
For all the trees are dressed
In lacy green, their arms upraised
Inviting birds to nest.
And from afar soft breezes come
Such sweet, perfumed air
And gently sway the trembling fern
And sweep away my care.

LIFE ALONG THE LITTLE WEKIVA

ACKNOWLEDGMENTS

With thanks and grateful appreciation we recognize the invaluable contribution of friends we've made while writing *Little Wekiva Memories*. Their stories, photos, spirit of generosity, and gift of time have made this book come to life.

Billy Ridgeback Bodie
Robert Brinton
Jason Byrne
Mayanne Downs
Ron and Lisa Huston
Rick Kilby
Miriam Oestricher
Sandra Smith Regal
Guy Rizzo
John Rountree
Robin Overstreet Sheldon
Marcia Harris Voorhees
Sue Tyndall
Parker Wilson

Thank You,

Bernadine Delafield and Chelsey Sugaski for reading the manuscript while Little Wekiva Memories was a work in progress. I appreciate your comments and editorial eye.

Tyler Shymske, for your attention to editorial details. Keith Newhouse, for your enthusiasm and support in bringing Little Wekiva Memories to the public through Hastings House Publishing.

NOTES

1. "Seminole History." Florida Department of State. Accessed January 28, 2024. https://dos.fl.gov/florida-facts/florida-history/seminole-history/.

2. "Sanlando Springs." SJRWMD, July 29, 2021. https://www.sjrwmd.com/waterways/springs/sanlando/.

3. Cierzniak, Libby. "Indianapolis Collected: The Fall of the House of Fletcher: Historic Indianapolis: All Things Indianapolis History." Historic Indianapolis, May 12, 2017. https://historicindianapolis.com/indianapolis-collected-the-fall-of-the-house-of-fletcher/.

4. Cronin, Richard Lee. "Central Florida Would-Be Titans: Elizabeth of Palm Springs, Seminole County, FL." *CitrusLAND*, 2015, https://citruslandfl.blogspot.com/2017/04/blog-series-central-florida-would-be.html.

5. Kilby, Rick. *Florida's healing waters: Gilded age Mineral Springs, Seaside Resorts, and Health Spas.* Gainesville, FL: University Press of Florida, 2020.

6. Cronin, Richard Lee. "Central Florida History Challenge: Part One." CitrusLAND, 2015, https://citruslandfl.blogspot.com/2020/08/central-florida-history-challenge-part.html.

7. Byrne, Jason. "Ginger Ale Springs." Florida History Blog, September 2024. https://floridahistoryblog.com/ginger-ale-springs/.

8. "Palm Springs." SJRWMD, July 28, 2021. https://www.sjrwmd.com/waterways/springs/palm-seminole/.

9. "Freeze Destroys Citrus in Florida." NOAA and the Preserve America https://www.weather.gov/media/tbw/paig/PresAmFreeze1894.pdf. Initiative.

10. "Slide into Springs Was Exciting Ride." *Orlando Sentinel*. September 29, 2000. https://www.orlandosentinel.com/news/os-xpm-2000-09-29-0009270585-story.html

11. Robison, Jim, and Orlando Sentinel Staff. "Kids Screamed Heads off on Best Waterslide in Area." Orlando Sentinel, October 25, 2018. https://www.orlandosentinel.com/2003/07/27/kids-screamed-heads-off-on-best-waterslide-in-area/.

12. Central Florida Society of Historical Preservation. Vol. Longwood of Images of America. Charleston, SC: Arcadia, 2001.

13. Follman, Joe and Buchanan, Richard. "Sanlando Spring." Springs Fever: A Field and Recreation Guide to 500 Florida Springs, 3rd Edition, 2018. http://www.thespringsfever.com/spr/Sanlando.html.

14. "Starbuck Spring." SJRWMD, June 30, 2017. https://www.sjrwmd.com/waterways/springs starbuck/.

15. Schumann, Christina. "Starbuck Spring." Florida Center for Community Design and Research. https://seminole.wateratlas.usf.edu/upload/documents/Starbuck.pdf.

16. "Ginger Ale Springs." SJRWMD, June 30, 2017. https://www.sjrwmd.com/waterways/springs/ginger-ale/.

17. "Pegasus Spring." SJRWMD, March 21, 2019. https://www.sjrwmd.com/waterways/springs/pegasus/.

18. Barnes, Steven. "Team Searches for Bubbly." Orlando Sentinel. February 24, 2005. https://www.orlandosentinel.com/2005/02/24/team-searches-for-bubbly/.

19. "St. Johns River Water Management District." SJRWMD, January 27, 2025. https://www.sjrwmd.com/.

20. "Friends of the Wekiva River." Friends of the Wekiva River. Accessed February 11, 2025. https://www.friendsofwekiva.org/.

21. "Sanlando (Hoosier) Springs." Longwood Historic Society. Accessed January 18, 2024. https://historiclongwood.com/sanlando-hoosier-springs/.

22. Khan, Nancy. Florida "senator" arrives at U.S. National Herbarium—The Plant Press, Vol 15, no.5, 18 Dec. 2012. Accessed April 20, 2023. https://nmnh.typepad.com/the_plant_press/2012/12/florida-senator-arrives-at-us-national-herbarium-.html.

23. Joanos, Jim. "Stars of Yesterday-Katherine Rawls." Seminole Spotlight, February 2008. https://www.nolefan.org/garnet/seminole20.html.

24. Overstreet family private collection of news clippings and memorabilia.

25. "Robinson, John E. Sr." Newspapers.com, 18 Dec. 1988, https://www.newspapers.com/article/the-orlando-sentinel-obituary-for-john-e/84167586/.

26. Byrne, Jason. "Petty's Market of Longwood." Florida History Blog, September 8, 2024. https://floridahistoryblog.com/pettys-market-of-longwood/.

27. "Cranes Roost Stirring Future Development Centers on Altamonte Springs Site." Orlando Sentinel, July 15, 2021. http://www.orlandosentinel.com/1985/05/19/cranes-roost-stirring-future-development-centers-on-altamonte-springs-site/.

28. "Johnny Tiger." Wikipedia, December 2, 2024. https://en.wikipedia.org/wiki/Johnny_Tiger.

29. "Epoch Has Grown with The Orlando Market." Orlando Sentinel, January 24,1994, https://www.orlandosentinel.com/1994/01/24/epoch-has-grown-with-the-orlando-market/

30. Dickinson, Joy Wallace, "Revered architect left mark on Central Florida." Orlando Sentinel, October 21, 2018, https://www.orlandosentinel.com/2018/10/21/revered-architect-left-mark-on-central-florida/

31. "The Springs—Longwood, FL Homes For Sale & Real Estate." Neighborhoods.com. Accessed February 11, 2025. https://www.neighborhoods.com/the-springs-longwood-fl.

BIBLIOGRAPHY

Barnes, Steven. "Team Searches for Bubbly." Orlando Sentinel, February 24, 2005, https://www.orlandosentinel.com/2005/02/24/team-searches-for-bubbly/.

Byrne, Jason. "Ginger Ale Springs." Florida History Blog, September 2024. https://floridahistoryblog.com/ginger-ale-springs/.

Byrne, Jason. "Petty's Market of Longwood." Florida History Blog, September 8, 2024. https://floridahistoryblog.com/pettys-market-of-longwood/.

Central Florida Society of Historical Preservation. Vol. Longwood of Images of America. Charleston, SC: Arcadia, 2001.

Cierzniak, Libby. "Indianapolis Collected: The Fall of the House of Fletcher: Historic Indianapolis: All Things Indianapolis History." Historic Indianapolis, May 12, 2017. https://historicindianapolis.com/indianapolis-collected-the-fall-of-the-house-of-fletcher/.

"Cranes Roost Stirring Future Development Centers on Altamonte Springs Site." Orlando Sentinel, July 15, 2021. http://www.orlandosentinel.com/1985/05/19/cranes-roost-stirring-future-development-centers-on-altamonte-springs-site/.

Cronin, Richard Lee. "Central Florida Would-Be Titans: Elizabeth of Palm Springs, Seminole County, FL." *CitrusLAND,* 2015, https://citruslandfl.blogspot.com/2017/04/blog-series-central-florida-would-be.html/.

Cronin, Richard Lee. "Central Florida History Challenge: Part One." CitrusLAND, 2015, https://citruslandfl.blogspot.com/2020/08/central-florida-history-challenge-part.html.

Dickinson, Joy Wallace, "Revered architect left mark on Central Florida." Orlando Sentinel, October 21, 2018, https://www.orlandosentinel.com/2018/10/21/revered-architect-left-mark-on-central-florida/

"Epoch Has Grown with The Orlando Market." Orlando Sentinel, January 24,1994, https://www.orlandosentinel.com/1994/01/24/epoch-has-grown-with-the-orlando-market/

Follman, Joe and Buchanan, Richard. "Sanlando Spring." Springs Fever: A Field and Recreation Guide to 500 Florida Springs, 3rd Edition, 2018. http://www.thespringsfever.com/spr/Sanlando.html.

"Friends of the Wekiva River." Friends of the Wekiva River. Accessed February 11, 2024. https://www.friendsofwekiva.org/.

"Freeze Destroys Citrus in Florida." NOAA and the Preserve America https://www.weather.gov/media/tbw/paig/PresAmFreeze1894.pdf. Initiative.

"Ginger Ale Springs." SJRWMD, June 30, 2017. https://www.sjrwmd.com/waterways/springs/ginger-ale/.

Images of America—Longwood, Central Florida Society for Historical Preservation, September, 25, 2001

Joanos, Jim. "Stars of Yesterday-Katherine Rawls." Seminole Spotlight, February 2008. https://www.nolefan.org/garnet/seminole20.html.

"Johnny Tiger." Wikipedia, December 2, 2024. https://en.wikipedia.org/wiki/Johnny_Tiger.

Khan, Nancy. Florida "senator" arrives at U.S. National Herbarium—The Plant Press, Vol 15, no.5, 18 Dec. 2012. Accessed April 20, 2023. https://nmnh.typepad.com/the_plant_press/2012/12/florida-senator-arrives-at-us-national-herbarium-.html.

Kilby, Rick. *Florida's healing waters: Gilded age Mineral Springs, Seaside Resorts, and Health Spas.* Gainesville, FL: University Press of Florida, 2020.

"Palm Springs." SJRWMD, July 28, 2021. *https://www.sjrwmd.com/waterways/springs/palm-seminole/.*

"Pegasus Spring." SJRWMD, March 21, 2019. https://www.sjrwmd.com/waterways/springs/pegasus/.

"Robinson, John E. Sr." Newspapers.com, 18 Dec. 1988, https://www.newspapers.com/article/the-orlando-sentinel-obituary-for-john-e/84167586/.

Robison, Jim, and Orlando Sentinel Staff. "Kids Screamed Heads off on Best Waterslide in Area." Orlando Sentinel, October 25, 2018. https://www.orlandosentinel.com/2003/07/27/kids-screamed-heads-off-on-best-waterslide-in-area/.

"Sanlando Springs." SJRWMD, July 29, 2021. https://www.sjrwmd.com/waterways/springs/sanlando/.

"Sanlando (Hoosier) Springs." Longwood Historic Society. Accessed January 18, 2024. https://historiclongwood.com/sanlando-hoosier-springs/.

Schumann, Christina. "Starbuck Spring." Florida Center for Community Design and Research. https://seminole.wateratlas.usf.edu/upload/documents/Starbuck.pdf.

"Seminole History." Florida Department of State. Accessed January 28, 2024. https://dos.fl.gov/florida-facts/florida-history/seminole-history/.

"Slide into Springs Was Exciting Ride." Orlando Sentinel. September 29, 2000.https://www.orlandosentinel.com/news/

"Starbuck Spring." SJRWMD, June 30, 2017. Accessed January 2024. https://www.sjrwmd.com/waterways/springs/starbuck/.

"St. Johns River Water Management District." SJRWMD, January 27, 2025. https://www.sjrwmd.com/.

"The Springs—Longwood, FL Homes For Sale & Real Estate." Neighborhoods.com. Accessed February 11, 2025. https://www.neighborhoods.com/the-springs-longwood-fl.

AUTHOR BIOGRAPHY

Nichole is an author, artist, and designer. As her three children grew into adulthood, she found herself taking on new adventures and pursuing different goals. Her two-day kayak trip on Minnesota's Gull Lake Chain and writing *Gull Lake Memories* helped renew her interest in writing. Travel adventures always inspire her. Her writing explores the idea that making memories in special places provides a firm foundation for life. "I've experienced what this can mean to a family. There are treasured spots we return to that bring us a sense of joy where we can remember what's important to us as a family and continue to build new memories that will sustain and connect us." She treasures time with her husband Jeff and their extended family.

Leif is studying political science and journalism at Southern Adventist University. While writing this book, he was a senior at Forest Lake Academy in Altamonte Springs, Florida. As editor of the school newspaper, *The Panther Press*, and writing for his school's alumni publications, he had an opportunity to reflect on the changing landscape of Central Florida. From an early age, Leif embraced the natural wonders all around him. Watching tadpoles become frogs, collecting shark teeth, and exploring the river were favorite pastimes. Uncovering the locations and histories of springs on the Little Wekiva has been an adventure, giving him a greater appreciation for the wild beauty of Florida.

How to Reach the Author

Nichole Delafield-Bromme is available for speaking engagements and events related to *Gull Lake Memories* and *Little Wekiva Memories*
nickibromme@gmail.com • www.nicholedelafield.com

About Newhouse Creative Group

Founded by Keith Newhouse and his father Mark Newhouse in 2017 on the principle that every story has a purpose, Newhouse Creative Group (NCG) aims to educate and innovate through its authors and their work.
Since then we've expanded to over 20 traditionally published authors and have helped numerous others with publishing and marketing services, online courses, coaching, consulting and more!

Whether looking for a novel to curl up with, an educational experience for your child, or a chance to live out your dream of being a writer, we hope that you'll become a part of the NCG family.

NCG is thrilled to be publishing Little Wekiva Memories and making it the first new title under the Hastings House name in over 10 years!

Newhouse Creative Group… Inspiring the Readers and Writers of Today and Tomorrow!

About Hastings House Publishers

Hastings House was founded in 1936 for the purpose of telling the world about America. Hastings has grown from a one-book, one author operation into an international publishing house with the rights to over 2700 books.

Since Walter Frese founded Hastings House (as he lived in the suburb of Hastings-on-Hudson), the publisher has been a part of some of the country's largest literary undertakings including:

- The WPA Writers' Project (A federally-funded New Deal program designed to keep writers from starving during the Great Depression)

- The American Guide (A 1948 one-volume guide to the United States which became Book-of-the-Month Club's most successful work up to that time)

- The American Procession Series (A significant literary venture of dramatic non-fiction books that center around the epic episodes in our history and cultural growth that until then had not been adequately told)

- The Daytrips Series (A series of travel guides that are still popular to this day)

Since Walter Frese retired in 1985, the firm was acquired by different publishing executives until it was moved to Florida by Peter Leers and his wife Dee. In 2024, Hastings House Publishers was acquired by Newhouse Creative Group in hopes of reinvigorating this almost 100 year old brand.

www.ingramcontent.com/pod-product-compliance
Lightning Source LLC
Chambersburg PA
CBRC101144030426
42337CB00009B/69